The Creative Heroine's Path

The Creative Heroine's Path

Live Your Creative Life

Julie Baldwin

Solevoluna
Boulder, Colorado

Copyright © 2019 by Julie Baldwin

All rights reserved. No part of this book may be reproduced by any means, or in any form, or stored in a database or retrieval system, without prior written permission of the publisher.

For information or inquiries, contact:

Solevoluna LLC
6525 Gunpark Drive, Suite 370-178
Boulder, CO 80301

www.solevoluna.com

The Creative Heroine's Path

ISBN 978-0-9987659-4-5 (hc)
ISBN 978-0-9987659-5-2 (pbk)

Second Edition

Solevoluna is a registered trademark of Solevoluna LLC.

Printed in the United States of America.

*To my father, Wayne Baldwin,
for his love, wisdom,
and grounded goodness.*

*To my mother, Ann Baldwin,
for her love, sharp mind,
and keen intuition.*

*To my husband, Dave Resch,
for his love, friendship, support,
and unfailing belief in me.*

Contents

Introduction v

Welcome to the Path

My Story. 3
What Is the Creative Heroine's Path? 6
On the Path 11
Living a Creative Life. 15

Awakening Your Creative Spirit

Creativity Is Abundant 25
Your Routine. 26
A Catalyst Wakes You Up 36

Dancing with the Muse

Creativity Is Messy. 57
Trusting the Potential in Chaos. 58
Tapping into Inspiration. 61

Responding to Your Calling

Creativity Is Spiritual 75
What Is Your Calling?. 77
Moving from Commitment to Devotion 86

Diving into the Mystery

Creativity Is Transformational. 100
Here Be Dragons. 102
Into the Abyss. 122
Discovering Your Vision. 140

Sharing Your Gifts

Creativity Is Inspirational 151
Finding Your Voice 155
Connecting with Kindred Spirits 163

Coming Home to Yourself

The Courage of a Heroine—or Hero 171
Take Compassionate Ownership 173
Stories You Tell Yourself 174
Mastering the Path 178
Finding Grace 186
List of Exercises 189
Acknowledgments 191
Credits 193

Disclaimer

Although the author and publisher have made every effort to ensure that the information in this book was correct at press time, the author and publisher do not assume, and hereby disclaim, any liability to any party for any loss, damage, or disruption caused by errors or omissions, whether such errors or omissions result from negligence, accident, or any other cause.

This book is not intended as a substitute for the medical advice of physicians. The reader should regularly consult a physician in matters relating to his or her health, and particularly with respect to any symptoms that may require diagnosis or medical attention.

Introduction

The Creative Heroine's Path is for anyone who longs to be more present, feel more alive, and be more consciously creative—both in how they respond in life and how they express their quirky, soulful brilliance.

You are creating all the time, *in* life and *of* life, with every single thing you do. This is your path to your most profound expression and your authentic life. Whether you are called to paint, write, sculpt, dance, sing, act—or cook, start a business, play an instrument—this path can help you make it real.

I use "heroine" rather than "hero" because the Creative Heroine's Path arises from the traditionally "feminine" *yin* energy of being.

Everything you do emerges directly from who you are, your life experiences, and how you see the world. Focusing only on the traditionally "masculine" *yang* energy of doing bypasses the necessary wisdom that informs your actions.

Just like the Chinese *taichi* symbol depicts those two energies as swirling parts of the whole, we move from being, to doing, to becoming. Our beings, who we are and what we value, direct our actions. What we learn from taking action (or choosing not to take action) influences who we are becoming. This is the creative ebb and flow in life.

Within the creative flow of your life, the Creative Heroine's Path gives a meaningful context for your creative expression. It illuminates the creative phases that are inherent in creative endeavor. When you consciously co-create with life, you take action from not just who you are, but from whom you want to become. Even when you take imperfect action, you move forward on your path.

Two of the biggest challenges you face on your path are choosing perspectives that support your best life, and dealing with your inner dragons—the negative voices that say you can't live a creative life.

Responding creatively—and positively—to those challenges directly influences the success of all you do.

This book contains exercises to help you go deeper and act from the core of who you are. Because when you take action from your authentic self, the magic of the world opens up to you. When you show up and make a real commitment to living your life authentically, you begin to create the life you want.

It's important to pause and take your time with the exercises. Write your answers in your journal or a notebook, so you can come back to them whenever you want to reconnect with what you learn about yourself on this path.

I developed the Creative Heroine's Path from my heart and soul, from the messy, zigzag path I've taken to living my true creative life. I wrote it to make sense of my own path, and to help others find and embark on their creative paths.

No one else can tell you how to make your own life, but I deeply hope this book helps you on your path. We light the way for each other.

Welcome to the Path

"Life isn't about finding yourself. Life is about creating yourself."
George Bernard Shaw

I had never been so tired in my life. After years of being overworked, dangerously over-stressed, and hanging on to daily life by the ends of my fingernails, something was very wrong.

But I didn't believe I could leave my job and survive, so I continued to work through my exhaustion. By the time I went to the doctor, I was at the edge of my endurance. I sobbed as I told her of the stress I felt, of being so tired I could barely do anything.

After multiple tests, I learned that the lower portions of both my lungs had a "cut glass" appearance. Although that scared me, I was assured it wasn't cancer. I seemed to have an infection, but what kind? I had no recent respiratory virus, which might have led to pneumonia. Was it actually pneumonia, or was it something else? I was referred to a pulmonary specialist.

While I waited for my appointment, I was unable to work, terrified that I was losing lung capacity from an unknown affliction. I scoured the internet, looking for a disease that matched my symptoms. All I found were dark possibilities.

I had to face the fact that I might not get better, that my condition would keep me from the hiking I loved, from traveling to faraway places—and worst, from writing my novel.

In a few short weeks, my life had narrowed from survival mode to just basic self-care. I was afraid that I'd squandered my chance to live the creative life I longed for—no, the creative life that I knew I was meant to live.

When I finally took a cab to see the specialist (too exhausted to drive myself), he told me that I probably had a bacterial infection. A week later, I had a bronchoscopy to remove a small amount of material from the bottom of my lungs, to determine what kind of bacteria caused it.

While I waited for the result, I knew I had to change my life.

But how?

CHAPTER 1

My Story

I am a writer who left her creative path to make a living. Writing is how I make sense of the world. It helps me to understand my thoughts and feelings on a deeper level. Through writing, I learn more about myself and others. I also write to remember—to express ideas and meaning—and to process experiences. It's what I need to do, and a big part of what I was meant to do.

When I want to meditate and ground myself, I paint. Playing with colors and shapes, creating images from a place deeper than words, is joyful and profound for me. And when my writing isn't flowing, getting out of my writer's brain and into my senses gets me back into the flow.

I also love to connect with and mentor creative, sensitive souls. I've learned that everyone needs help at times; no one truly does it alone. Seeing the gifts of my fellow human beings, and helping them unfurl those gifts to blossom in the world, is inspiring and meaningful.

My calling is to create, connect, and serve. Only by living my own authentic and creative life can I help others do the same. And yet, I don't always succeed at staying on my path. Navigating life is a process, an art in itself.

I think of my wise inner self as the North Star that I try to steer by. Sometimes, my soul's wisdom is the spark in the darkness that keeps me from sinking. Other times, it is a clear beacon that I steer by. Still other times, it is the luminous wisdom that both grounds and buoys me in my daily experiences.

Where I Left the Path

While making my way in the world, I betrayed myself.

I came to believe that to survive, I had to give up on expressing my true self. I thought I had to put away my calling to use my greatest gifts, because who would want what I had to offer, anyway? I believed that living a creative life was only for a few special people, and that I was not one of them.

I am embarrassed to admit that, in part, I didn't live a creative life because I knew it would demand big changes of me. I would need to let go of the security I felt in the comfortable income that my not-so-creative job provided. And I would have to change my status quo life that, ironically, I didn't want anyway.

But spiritually, I wasn't ready to make those changes. I was clinging to the life preserver of the material world, even as I longed to dive deep into the mystery of existence.

Our beliefs shape the trajectory of our lives.

Instead of devoting myself to my creative writing, I got a job as a technical writer. I was not yet ready—or willing—to answer the call. How do I know? Because I could have made a living and worked seriously on my writing. But I didn't make the commitment to give my creative expression the priority it deserved.

No matter how many excuses I made for not following my calling, it was my choice.

Self-betrayal is a universal experience of being human. It's one way that we learn, on a deeper level, what really matters to us. You learn who you are after feeling deep loss, facing the truth, and finding the path to reclaim yourself.

Even though I wasn't fully doing my true work in the world, I tried to keep my dreams alive. I joined writing groups and I took independent courses, to grow as a writer. I painted watercolors. I found expression for my empathy—and my calling to serve and mentor—by becoming a manager, to support others in their growth and dreams.

But despite the relative comfort in my daily life, it wasn't enough.

Eventually, not following my true path took a toll on me. I got sick. And then, when the company where I worked for 19 years was acquired, I lost my job.

My illness and layoff were the catalysts that helped me see it was time to make a change. A big change.

Finding My Way Again

It has not been a straight and easy path.

Over and over, I had to decide whether I would follow the path of growth and change, or give up. One of the most difficult things I had to relearn, as a person and an artist, was how to find balance—between caring deeply and letting go of my attachment to outcomes, and between working hard on a blueprint and following my intuition.

Along the way, I discovered something: like any endeavor, writing a book is a spiritual path, if you put your soul into it.

Writing this book required learning, stretching myself, and facing my fears. It required deep self-assessment, and dealing with my "inner dragons." It revealed insights that were waiting for me to bring them into the light. And finally, it required me to show up and be seen, in ways that I was afraid to do just a couple years ago.

I am still in the process of reclaiming myself, in a holistic way, beyond my art. Finding my voice and sharing my vision in this book is part of that journey. Now I see the arc of my life—and my successes and failures along the way—in the context of the Creative Heroine's Path.

CHAPTER 2

What Is the Creative Heroine's Path?

The Creative Heroine's Path is a way of living that honors and supports your creativity.

Because life is inherently creative, you are constantly co-creating with the universe. When you respond to situations with the question, "What can I create from this?" you open up your life to create more consciously.

The path provides a structure to the natural flow of life and creativity in the form of a story, to help you understand and make the most of your experiences. It provides a meaningful context for the growth and challenges you experience when you commit to your art.

By owning your part in creating your life, and by understanding the creative flow, you will find the right path for yourself. Your path is not a straight line, or a smooth and predictable cycle, and that's okay. It evolves as you do.

My path evolved as I was trying to make sense of my hopscotch journey toward living my creative life. When I looked for context to help me understand my creative process, I found it in:

- The five-act structure of the dramatic arc of storytelling, which is echoed in the five distinct phases of the path.
- The deeper meaning in Joseph Campbell's work on the archetypal hero's journey, which brings in the component of spiritual growth.

The Classic Story Arc

Dramatic structure is a larger context given to events, through story. It presents the heroine's experiences in an order that makes sense of the flow of life, revealing meaning that she is often unable to see while experiencing it.

When applied to your creative endeavors, or your life, the story arc helps you see the bigger context, and the connections between events. This is helpful whenever you're feeling lost, unsure of which steps to take next.

The Archetypal Hero's Journey

Through his studies of mythology, Joseph Campbell developed his concept of the hero's journey. It parallels the five-part story arc: the hero experiences loss, goes on a quest, commits to his calling, meets challenges and overcomes obstacles, and finally returns to his tribe with deeper knowledge.

Campbell's special contribution was to reveal this archetypal experience as a framework for spiritual growth. The hero's journey is more than an external experience—it is also an inner journey of transformation that parallels the outer journey. The hero becomes the person he needs to be to meet the challenges of his outer journey.

Learning about this was life-changing for me, because it helped me to understand the context of my experiences—especially the dark times.

Tapping into the spiritual meaning of your path brings you courage and motivation for each step you need to take.

The Path

The Creative Heroine's Path winds through the organic ebb and flow of the creative process. It reveals the creative process in story form. It is also a way of being, of looking at life, that helps you partner with the creative flow.

Think of it as a kind of filter, through which the confusing messiness of creativity—and life—coalesces into a meaningful whole.

When viewed as a story, the phases in the creative process flow from one to another, like acts and scenes in a play. The story provides meaningful context that otherwise you can't always see when you're in the middle of it. When you learn to recognize where you are, you can consciously move through each creative phase.

The Creative Flow

In the context of a story, my experience of the creative flow tends to unfold like this:

Act One:
> In the middle of the routine of everyday life, I begin to feel restless. Something is awakening, and wants to be expressed, or brought into the world, through ink or paint on paper.

Act Two:
> When I first begin to follow my impulse to write or paint, nothing is clear. But if I stay with it long enough, I begin to surf a wave of energy. I feel inspired, and my writing or painting begins to take form.

Act Three:
> Within the emerging form, I begin to sense what is calling me within what I am doing—to capture a feeling in words, or to blend color in a way that simply brings me contentment.

I know the calling requires me to go deeper, stay present, and focus. This is where I commit or let go. When I commit and act on that, a deeper devotion to what I am creating rises up in me and propels me forward.

Act Four:

After focusing for a while, the energy fades. The wave drops and pulls back, and I dive beneath the surface. This is where I need my devotion, along with courage, to face my inner dragons in the deep.

When I accept the grief, the unknown, or whatever flows through me, I find treasure—my vision—in a pearl of an insight, an evocative color flowing from the brush, or words that resonate with the emotion they try to convey.

Act Five:

When I risk being vulnerable, to share what I've written or painted, I feel seen—and sometimes understood. I begin to discern the false notes from the true. My voice strengthens and becomes more my own, as my confidence rises.

When I connect with kindred spirits by sharing my gifts and experiencing theirs, I feel both a sense of completion and fresh inspiration.

The overarching story gives me a kind of map, so I can see where I am at any time. Instead of feeling at the mercy of whatever state I'm in, I see the process with a deeper level of acceptance and understanding. I know that I'm living part of a bigger meaning, and that the difficult states are as essential as the ones I love to be in the most.

I used to believe that I was either creating or not creating. Strictly speaking, that's true. When I'm in my routine, or in the abyss, I'm not outwardly creating. I used to view those times as "failures"—or my inner dragon did (more about inner dragons later).

However, when I look at creativity holistically, I see that each phase is meaningful and plays a role.

Sometimes, I need to be in my routine to recharge my creative juju, even when I wish I was tapped into inspiration and creating. If I was creating all the time, I'd burn out.

Other times, I'm in the abyss, feeling lost and hopeless, wishing I had a clear sense of my vision. But being lost is the prelude to finding my way, and accepting that as a necessary part of the creative flow helps me move through it to the next phase.

Instead of fighting the state I'm in, or wallowing in negativity about not being where I want to be (and it always feels like it will be that way forever, doesn't it?), now I understand that even when I think I'm out of the flow, I am just experiencing an ebb in the overall creative process.

Being more conscious of the phases in the creative flow has given me the freedom and power to experience my creative life more fully, and to bring it more alive each day.

That is the gift I offer to you with this book: the ability to choose to live more creatively, in all ways possible.

CHAPTER 3

On the Path

Creativity is a powerful process, a doorway into the mystery of your own inner life and existence. Through the meaningful ritual of a creative practice, you use your experiences and imagination to create your art and your life.

Of course, creativity itself is largely unconscious. That's why it sometimes feels so magical to bring your vision into existence from a deep place. But when you are more intentional about choosing the perspectives and actions that support rather than sabotage your creative dreams, you can build a creative life for yourself.

You are creating all the time, co-creating with the universe, deliberately or otherwise. We're all just making it up as we go along, intentionally or not.

Being more conscious of the creative flow in which you swim helps you optimize the freedom and power that emerge when you take responsibility for what you create in—and of—your life. You can directly support your own genius: your unique contribution to this world.

The Creative Heroine's Path supports living a more consciously creative life. The path unfolds like a story. Because your experience of the creative flow is not linear, the story helps you see the natural ebb and flow of your creativity within a bigger context.

Like a play, the Creative Heroine's Path contains distinct phases—or acts—that focus on specific states of being, and outer actions that move you toward growth, within the natural ebb and flow of your creativity.

Growth isn't linear, and you revisit each phase over and over as you create something new. The key is to recognize where you are so you can optimize your experience and find your way forward.

The flow of creativity begins with an awakening, moves to a dance, evokes a response, compels a deep dive, and ends with sharing what you have created.

Phase One: Awakening Your Creative Spirit

When your creative spirit awakens, you transcend the routine of your everyday life through the spark of a catalyst.

Routine

Your routine is the starting place for the path. When you're in your routine, you're moving through your usual habits and reactions. You're attending to the minutiae of daily life.

Catalyst

Then, a catalyst sparks a creative insight, or an outer change occurs. Something quickens inside you. You know you must create something new in your life, but you might be unsure what to think or do about it—yet.

Phase Two: Dancing with the Muse

Your initial dance movements feel chaotic and confusing. But when you trust the process, the muse brings inspiration and creativity. You begin to create your art.

Chaos

When you begin to create, nothing is clear. You've got lots of ideas but no direction. You might be jumping from project to project, never settling on one long enough to complete it. Or you may feel overwhelmed and unsure where to start.

Inspiration

When the muse steps in, you feel plugged in to the universe. You're writing, painting, designing, singing—bringing something into the world. You are excited and inspired!

Phase Three: Responding to Your Calling

When you respond to your calling by honoring your commitment to yourself, you discover the deeper meaning in what you are creating. You answer your calling with devotion.

Calling

Once your creation begins to take shape, you sense a deeper calling within. Something clicks in your awareness. You know this is what you are meant to do. You feel passionate, purposeful, and powerful. You're planning and working things out.

Devotion

When you commit to what you're creating long enough, it deepens into devotion. You're tapped into why you are creating, and you feel more committed than ever before. Your devotion carries you through as you work on your creative project, even when it's difficult.

Phase Four: Diving into the Mystery

When you dive into the mystery, you're going deeper into the vast ocean of your experience—both conscious and subconscious. You're venturing into the dark, pathless forest, searching for insight and deeper wisdom. You're braving the abyss to discover your vision.

Abyss

When you're in the abyss, your energy drops; things feel bleak. You believe you can't do it. You feel blocked, despairing, hopeless, depressed, anxious, lost, or listless.

Vision

When you see your vision, a shift has happened; you're seeing from a new vista. You see clearly what to do or how things fit together. You're excited and experiencing insights!

Phase Five: Sharing Your Gifts

When you share your gifts, you're developing your voice and unique talents as you connect with kindred spirits.

Voice

As you share your unique way of expressing your creativity with others, you hear your own voice more clearly. You might be sharing your creativity with a select few. You feel vulnerable, scared, excited—or all three—but your confidence is growing as you refine your creative expression.

Connection

When you connect with a community of kindred spirits, you feel energized, appreciated, seen, and heard. You realize how much your gifts matter. And experiencing the creativity of others brings you fresh inspiration.

CHAPTER 4

Living a Creative Life

What is a creative life?

A creative life is grounded in being present—in noticing, seeing deeply, and being open to your intuition. It brings you glimpses of how things are connected, informing your life and your art.

A creative life is centered by your inner wisdom and aligns with your deepest values. You are the author of your life.

You build a creative life through responding creatively. When your life doesn't go as planned, you ask, "What can I create from this?" You build the spiritual resilience that allows you to make choices that move you toward your dreams.

A creative life supports your growth in—and through—your creative expression. You develop a regular creative practice, and you develop yourself as you develop your art.

In a creative life, you take time to experience the creativity of others. Your life is steeped in appreciation of the gifts that touch you, inspiring your own creative expression.

In a creative life, you are living life to the fullest, however that looks for you.

Focusing on What Matters

Living creatively means being fully present in your life. There's a Buddhist belief that whatever you do, if you do it with full presence, it's like praying. I believe this. There is a spiritual intensity that pulses beneath the visible world, and we enter it when we focus.

I think that is why we need to check out now and then, as when our inner autopilot gets us to the grocery store, without noticing each turn of the drive. But if we're not careful, we can sleepwalk through much of our lives, especially when we're unhappy with our circumstances. As artists, we need to stay awake. We need to experience our aliveness to consciously create from and in our lives.

When I am painting a picture or writing a story, I'm focused in the moment. Especially when writing, I feel tapped into something bigger than myself. I feel more alive. It's like a hidden energy rises and expands in me, the spirit in flight, when I'm focused and creating.

But presence is also a stake, grounding you in the depth of rich details, while you lift off in flights of imagination. It helps you remember what matters.

Staying present, especially during difficult times, takes practice. The more you do it, the stronger you become. Building that strength is a spiritual benefit of creativity. The more you experience the presence of your own creative focus, the more you bring deeper insights into your art and your life.

Charting Your Own Course

Everyone is full of advice: Do this, not that. Get a degree, learn a trade, go into science. Play it safe. Take risks.

There is no right or wrong answer, only the best creative choice for you.

You get to set your unique course, as you respond to what crosses your path, because you are the heroine—the protagonist—of your own life story. You are the author of your life, creating from the core of yourself and responding to outer events like an improvisational musician in a band.

I won't tell you to quit your job to pursue your bliss, or find a steady job and work until you retire. I know of examples where each of those strategies worked well, or didn't, because of the deeper callings of the people involved.

My father had a career in a government job, doing something that he loved: working with airplanes. That job gave him more security than he would have had working in the private sector, and he was able to retire early and continue doing the things he enjoyed.

My friend's father worked at a job he hated for years. Before he could retire, to do more of what he loved—running marathons—he died suddenly of a brain aneurism.

My brother-in-law quit his job as an art teacher, and built up his clientele for his stunning watercolor paintings, allowing him to make a living through his creative expression.

I know many people—including myself—who practiced their creative expression in their free time, while working a "regular" job to support themselves and their families. I did that for over 20 years, but it wasn't enough. Now, I'm taking a more creative, intuitive path to make a living. Ironically, I'm taking risks now that I was unprepared to take when, in hindsight, it could have been "easier." But life is never a straight line.

There are no guarantees in a world as complex as ours. But as I work to create a life that is more aligned with my deepest values and that supports me to express my truest vision, I feel like I am coming home to myself.

You are already charting your own course. Don't do it by default.

Responding Creatively

Responding creatively—rather than reacting unconsciously—gives you the freedom to create your most meaningful, authentic life.

When you respond creatively, you notice your initial reaction to a situation, but you choose to act (or take no action) in alignment with your true values, with what is right. Your reaction reveals what you value; your response reveals what you want to create from that value. When you look beneath the surface or take a wider view, you may discover a meaning that is bigger than your initial impression.

You also stay open to possibilities, honestly assess where you are, and listen to your intuition for ways to solve problems—as you build your resilience.

Open to the Mystery

When you respond creatively, you understand that you don't always know the answer, or the outcome.

When I'm feeling lost, I often ask God, or the universe, or my higher self—use whatever concept feels true to you—for help in seeing the right path for me.

Usually, a sense of calm comes over me. Often, a new thought emerges from the fog.

And always, when I acknowledge the deep mystery of being alive, I am in awe.

Acceptance

When you respond creatively, you might wish things were different, but you accept reality, which allows you to work with what you have.

Instead of trying to "force" an outcome (and how well does that ever work, anyway?), you look for what you might need to learn, and adjust your course accordingly. A winding path may actually be the quickest way to get to where you want to be. There may be something you need to experience to prepare you for the next part of your path. Or something that wakes you up to discover that you want to be on a different path altogether.

Acceptance does not mean giving up, or not asserting your positive power in your life. It often means forgiving yourself or others for mistakes so you can move on, so you can take imperfect action. I've wasted a lot of time not starting, because I felt so behind already. (Try to follow that logic!)

But when I finally took a clear look at where I was, and accepted that, I was able to begin taking small steps. By writing a weekly blog, I slowly built my creative practice to the point where I could write this book.

Curiosity

When you respond creatively, you look for the clues that life brings you. Staying open, curious, and conscious goes a long way toward helping you learn what you need to know, sooner.

The more you listen to the whispers of your intuition, the more you trust your own inner wisdom. When you choose to view life through new perspectives, you can circumvent your old, entrenched reactivity. This brings incredible peace and optimism.

Expressing Your Creativity

I've been creative in different ways, all my life. As a little girl, I wrote stories, illustrated them with stick figures, and bound them in shiny burgundy cardboard. (My favorite story was about a catfish who gave loud parties in a farmer's pond. The farmer was angry until the catfish invited him to join in.)

On the back porch, I put on plays using my dolls and stuffed animals. I sang. I played the piano. I made things out of mud and decorated them with colored chalk. I'm pretty sure I still have a crude mud bowl somewhere!

As children, we are naturally creative. It's how we explore, and how we express ourselves. It's how we make sense of our world, and how we are in the world.

In fact, I believe that creative exploration, expression, and play is not only our natural way of being, it is essential to our happiness and growth. Conscious play with the universe helps us tap into the core of ourselves.

And it's the way to create a life aligned with your true self.

There are myriad ways that your natural creativity can get neglected or shut down:

Lack of support and appreciation, or worse, being shamed. Perhaps a teacher criticized your art, or family members believed making your art was a waste of time.

Not wanting to compete. Perhaps a sibling was considered to be the creative one, and you took on a different role in your family.

Making a living in a job that drains you. Perhaps you don't even believe you have the right to create a life that fits who you really are.

Taking care of others, and the busyness of life. You might believe you're being "selfish" if you do something creative rather than mow the lawn.

Self-doubt, perfectionism, and self-sabotage. You might believe that you have to be an expert, or a genius, for your creative expression to be valid or worthwhile.

Insufficient structure and habits. You might fear that too much structure will stifle your creativity, so you don't structure your life to support it.

Fear of the unknown. You might fear diving deeply into your subconscious, both because of how you might feel during the dive, and what you might bring up from the depths.

Over-responsibility. Perhaps you don't want to waste materials, or time or money, so you don't even begin. You don't play, try new things, or get words on paper.

If your creativity has been shut down, this is the perfect time to start it up again!

Keeping the Faith

You are gifted and creative. You see and experience the world in your own quirky, unique way, and you want to share your vision with others. If responsibilities (and even self-sabotage) pull you in every other direction, away from your creative dreams, don't give up!

You are the creative heroine—or hero—of your life. You are the author of your own story.

It can be tempting to play small, to hide your gifts. Don't do it!

It's time to grow into who you need to be, to live the creative life you are meant to live.

A Word About Late Bloomers

Years ago, when I was in my thirties, and despondent that I had wasted part of my life, my dream therapist told me that everyone is on their own timetable. When we talked about the things that held me back, he said the wonderful thing about "late bloomers" is that all the energy spent holding back is available to shoot you forward, like an arrow.

Imagine your spirit as the archer. You may have been pulling back on the bow of your potential for a long time. It can be exhausting, but now that you're ready—and you are, or you wouldn't be reading this book—you have all that stored energy at your disposal.

If you're approaching middle age or beyond, you actually have more psychic energy behind your calling than a 20-year-old.

Think about that. Trust it. Have faith that you will make amazing progress toward your creative dreams and goals.

All you need to do is take imperfect action, one step at a time.

Experiencing the Gifts of Others

I used to think I had to stop reading novels and short stories when I was writing, so as not to be influenced by them. Over time, I discovered that I needed to nourish my creativity by experiencing the creative expression of others. I've literally seen my own stories dry up from lack of outside inspiration.

How many times have you been deeply touched by a song, a novel, or a movie that made you feel less alone? Or that sparked an idea? Or that inspired your own creative expression?

Experiencing the creative expression of others is a source of inspiration and germination for your own creativity. Julia Cameron calls these "artist dates." Take your inner artist to an exhibition, a play, a concert, a poetry reading. When you nourish your creativity, you awaken a deep part of yourself. And it is essential to living a creative life.

Awakening Your Creative Spirit

*"And you? When will you begin
that long journey into yourself?"*
Rumi

When I developed an infection in my lungs, I was somewhat disabled by my illness. But I was even more disabled by my perspective: I felt stuck and hopeless.

Thankfully, about a year earlier, I had begun working with a life coach to try to find a new direction. I knew I wanted to write, paint, and travel, and I had an innate desire to help others. I wasn't yet sure how I was going to combine those callings, but I decided to begin with completing the training and certification to be a life coach.

On my journey, I discovered how powerful a change in perspective is—and how difficult it can be to change. I was faced with a challenge: how could I help others to pursue their creative dreams, if I still didn't believe mine were possible?

Ethically and practically, I couldn't.

Before I could help others claim their creative lives, I needed to reclaim my own. I had a lot of personal growth ahead of me. And I had no idea how I would do it, other than to stay as conscious as possible and put one foot in front of the other.

Then, in perfect timing, I was laid off from the company where I worked. It was exactly what I needed: the final push to embark on my own Creative Heroine's Path.

And that undiagnosed lung infection? It eventually cleared up on its own.

CHAPTER 5

Creativity Is Abundant

Life is not about getting; it's about creating.

Abundance isn't about having more stuff. Some of my most abundant experiences in life happen when I'm living out of a suitcase—exploring, writing, and painting.

Creativity is making something new. A painting, a poem, a life. It begins with an impulse and an idea. You use your experience and materials, and take imperfect action to bring your idea into being, creating something that only you could make.

You may think imagination is passive, but in a creative world, it is anything but. Your imagination is the first step to manifesting. Through it, you co-create with the universe.

Your thoughts are extremely powerful. That's why your perspective is so important. What you think about, you create. I don't mean magically; you have to take action. But how you see the world, what you believe is possible—even what you believe you deserve—colors what you see, how you see it, and the choices and actions you take.

CHAPTER 6

Your Routine

You're in your routine when you're on autopilot and doing any kind of activity—mundane or not—around the basics of living life: making breakfast, commuting, cleaning house.

Being in your routine is more than what you're doing: it's how you're being. When you're in your routine, you're also living from your default point of view: and that directly affects what you create in your life.

When your routine includes rituals that ground you—like brewing a pot of tea in the morning—it's comforting. When you're routinely honoring your values—such as making a healthy meal for your family—your day is made of moments of meaning that center you.

But when your routine fills your days with activities that have lost their meaning, or that crowd out other meaningful parts of your life—like your creative expression—it can feel tedious and frustrating.

The Comfort Zone

Your routine is a comfort zone, even when it's stressful and uncomfortable.

Comfort zones aren't good or bad. After all, they are structures you've built to support your life. But if you stay in them when they no longer serve you—like I did for the last several years in my job—they become ruts.

There's a wonderful, simple map of possibilities, and it looks like this:

Where the magic happens!

Your comfort zone

Look at the small comfort zone circle, and all the space outside of it. I love it because it looks like our comfort zones are islands, and the magic is offshore, in a place where perhaps we can't see land, and we don't know what's next. (Yes, I may be a bit of a romantic.)

How do you do it? How do you step out of the boundaries of your little haven, off the firm island and into the watery realm? First, you need a boat, or just a bit of imagination.

Imagine yourself in a sailboat, floating quietly, absorbing each moment as it enters your consciousness and echoes deep inside you, subtly changing the shoreline of your mind.

Imagine hoisting the sails and gliding through the unknown, adjusting and adapting as your vessel rises and dips with the waves. You can achieve whatever you are called on to do, or to be.

It takes meaning to fill your sails, ritual to center you, and support—abilities and allies—to leave the "safety" of the harbor.

Because here's the truth: change is inevitable. If you don't choose it, life brings it. I clung to my old life until a health issue woke me up, and being laid off from my job forced further change upon me.

When you are clear about what you really want, understand how to center and ground yourself, and know your assets and allies, you're in a better position to weather any storm of change.

And here's the wonderful miracle of it all: when you move out of your comfort zone, you expand your comfort zone. Your inner and outer worlds grow bigger. You realize you have more room to experience your precious life, and your confidence in yourself grounds you in that expanded life.

You can do it after all!

What Matters to You?

When you want or need something beyond the familiar boundaries of your current life, that motivation is the force that pulls you out of your comfort zone.

Years ago, I applied for a scholarship to take a creative writing class in Tuscany. I received a very nice rejection letter, saying the scholarship had been awarded to someone else. I was disappointed, but glad that I tried.

Then, just a few weeks before the class, I received an email from the program director telling me that the scholarship recipient had to decline it—and would I like the spot?

Yes!

But there was an obstacle: I didn't have a passport, and it would take several weeks to get one.

I was not going to let that stop me. My soul longed for this experience. I remember saying that I was going to Italy if I had to swim across the ocean! Luckily, I found out about a company that expedited the passport process by hand-delivering paperwork, and walking it to all the required government offices. I acted quickly, and my passport came in time!

When I arrived in Tuscany, I was alone and I didn't speak Italian. My companions were a phrasebook, an independent spirit, and absolute commitment to experiencing something new.

What motivated me? I knew that underneath all the surface obstacles was the chance to see the world with new eyes. And by new eyes, I don't just mean the vision of someone changed by her experience; I also mean the way we look at the world as children, when it's new and full of discoveries, eyes filled with wonder.

And I did just that. I walked along the Ponte Vecchio, saw the statue of David, and gazed through the Uffizi's paned windows at the Arno as the sun descended in the sky.

I wrote at a desk beneath a wide stone windowsill in an old Tuscan villa. In the mornings, I watched the misted hills rolling green and soft in the golden sunrise. It was absolutely wonderful!

No matter how much you plan, you have to respond to the unexpected. Acting in alignment with what matters to you gives you the strength and motivation to do more.

When you are aligned with your values, it grounds you in a context that makes sense. From there, you can decide what to do.

Exercise: Know What You Really Want

1. What do you long to do?
2. What do you really want?

    This isn't about what you are "supposed" to want, but what you truly want in the secret places of your soul.
3. If time, money, and responsibilities were not an issue, what would you do?
4. Why would you do it?

Centering Through Ritual

Rituals are small, everyday things you do that are infused with meaning. For me, a ritual—such as making tea with breakfast in the morning, using my favorite teapot and mug—grounds me in my day.

Just like infusing water with tea leaves, you can infuse action with intention. When you open the drapes in the morning, you are raising the curtain to begin the action of your day. When you close the drapes at night, you are signaling the end of your day. It's time to stop checking email, stop working, and let your inner clock wind down for the night.

And, to paraphrase Caroline Casey, "when you sweep out the floor, you can also sweep out the past."

It's so easy to get frazzled and approach everyday tasks as nuisances that take you away from what you really want to be doing. Frankly, I spent years thinking that way. What a waste.

Now, I remember to slow down and focus. When I have breakfast in the morning, I light a candle to remind myself to be grateful for the food on my table and all the blessings in my life. The beauty of the flickering candlelight connects me to the spiritual side of my life.

Exercise: **Develop Supportive Rituals**

1. What little rituals do you already do every morning or evening, or when you're doing your creative practice, that help center you?
2. What rituals can you build into your day to remind you to slow down and focus?

    For example, lighting a candle, brewing coffee or tea, or taking a walk.

Calling on Your Assets and Allies

The support available to us is as wide as the horizon: part ourselves, part others, part universe. You have more support available to you than you realize. You have skills and abilities that will support you on your path. And you have allies who believe in you and will help you, if you ask.

Recognizing Your Assets

Because of my detour from my creative path into technical writing, and people and project management, I gained skills that helped me to write this book and create my business.

Life is creative, and so are you. You have abilities that will support your authentic path.

When you need to learn new skills, you have a world of information at your fingertips: YouTube videos, webinars, online courses, and reference material on the web.

Exercise: **Discover Your Creative Assets**

1. Begin a list of your skills and abilities.
2. Ask others to tell you what skills and abilities they see in you.

    You can send an email to trusted friends and family, or ask them in person. Then, sit back and read, or listen. Hear what they are telling you. Let yourself appreciate the qualities that others value in you.

    Appreciating your own gifts helps you tap into your inner authority, and your power to create in the world.
3. Add the skills and abilities your friends and family told you about that are not already on your list.
4. Think of a situation when you had to grow and learn and stretch yourself, when you did something well and were proud of yourself. What skills and abilities did you use?
5. Complete the list with any new skills and abilities you discover.
6. Read the list.

    Read it again.

    Keep the list handy for times when you doubt yourself. You are so much more than you give yourself credit for!

Who Are Your Allies?

I've found that most people want to be helpful, and surprising coincidences conspire to support me when I take responsibility for my part, step out of my comfort zone, and keep my perspective open to possibilities.

I am grateful for supportive friends and family. Counseling has helped me many times in my life. I've done dream analysis with the help of a Jungian analyst. And I've invested in getting support from life and business coaches. No one does it alone.

When you need more support, get it.

Exercise: **Know Your Allies**

1. What support do you have for stepping out of the familiar and growing into the next phase of your life?

   Who are your champions, your cheerleaders, your co-conspirators?

2. How can you get the support you need?

   Would working with a counselor, a coach, or a spiritual advisor help you right now?

   If your answer is yes, reach out.

What Gives You Courage?

Many times, we know what we want, but we talk ourselves out of it because it seems like there are too many obstacles. The first can be facing our own fears of stepping outside of the known and into the possible. You call on your own courage when, despite your worst fears, you step out of your comfort zone anyway.

And remember, at the edges of fear, there's excitement!

On another trip to Italy, I had to take a *vaporetto* from my hotel in Venice to Marco Polo Airport for an early morning departure. It was still night when I stepped out of the hotel onto the cobbled street and walked to the end, where the black water of the canal lapped against the old stones.

I was alone on a dark, deserted street in Venice, in the middle of the night. I was unsure whether the water taxi would even show up. Yet it is one of my most exquisite memories.

The sky was clear, with a nearly full moon. The white stones of a nearby building glowed in the moonlight.

It was quiet. Nothing moved but a slight breeze. No footfalls or voices echoed in the maze of stone and water. I felt like I was the only person in the sleeping city.

Eventually, a vaporetto pulled up. I was the only passenger. We sped through the Grand Canal, passing the illuminated old buildings under a moonlit sky, and I arrived at the airport in plenty of time to catch my flight.

What if I had not summoned the courage to take that trip? All that wonder and beauty would exist out in the world, but not in my own experience.

Exercise: **Celebrate Your Courage**

1. When have you mustered the strength to do something that felt a little—or very—scary to you?
2. What helped you to call on your natural courage when you needed it?
3. What did you learn about yourself from that experience?
4. Celebrate that you did it. It matters.

Your Lodestar for This Path

I believe that we are meant to live a life in alignment with our deepest values, and to use our unique gifts in service of those values.

Your values motivate you and give you courage to live your authentic life.

I used to think of my life as being divided into:

- What I had to do, but didn't want to do.
- What I had to do, and wanted to do.
- What I wanted to do.

Although I was determined to do more of what I wanted to do, you can guess what got the most attention: whatever appeared most urgent at the moment. In other words, things I had to do, or thought I had to do. Things like my job, and the minutiae of daily life.

I hated the way my life felt. I'd segmented and fragmented it in ways that only brought me disappointment. That's not how I wanted to live. I wanted a way of life—a way of being and looking at the world—that felt more natural to me. I wanted a way of life that supported and facilitated who I wanted to become.

I discovered that I needed a point of reference, a *lodestar*, to help me both find my direction, and stay on my path.

So, I examined my priorities, and re-committed to what mattered most. Taking a look at what I really valued—and committing to it because it mattered so much to me—has helped me stay on my path, even when old habits threaten to pull me off of it.

This is the lodestar that I created when I began to write this book:

A lodestar is different than a goal. It's not a destination; it is more like a signpost or a compass directing you to follow your deepest values.

As you begin your path, you will focus on what matters to you, and why it matters. Just like I did, you'll need your own lodestar to find your way. Your lodestar might be a principle, something you value, an interest, or even a person—your muse—that inspires or guides you.

Exercise: **Find Your Lodestar**

This exercise helps you identify an image or a phrase to inspire and guide you on your path.

1. In a few sentences, describe a special, peak experience in your life.

   It could be the birth of your child, a special vacation, achieving a goal, experiencing synchronicity—any moment or time period that was deeply meaningful to you.

2. What made this peak experience so meaningful?

   For example: family, spirituality, adventure, teamwork, relationships, creativity—or whatever you value that you experienced.

3. Which of those things that you value feels the most essential to you right now? (Choose more than one if you want!)

4. Say what you value out loud. What image or phrase comes to mind?

   For example:
   - "Family" might evoke the image of your children or the phrase, "Home is where the heart is."
   - "Adventure" might evoke the image of a group of skydivers falling together in a circle or the phrase, "Go for it!"

5. As simply or ornately as you wish, create a visual representation of what you value, using images, words, or both.

6. Put your lodestar somewhere you will see it every day to remind you of the experiences you want to create in your life.

7. Regularly, ask yourself whether the choices you're making and how you're spending your time are in alignment with your lodestar. If not, redirect your course.

CHAPTER 7

A Catalyst Wakes You Up

When it's time to grow, you move from the comfort zone of the familiar, through the doorway of a catalyst, into unfamiliar territory.

A catalyst is an inner or outer change that brings a call for action:
- You become aware that something in your life no longer means what it used to. You have outgrown something in your life.
- You are thrust into change through an external event—an illness, losing a job, or losing a relationship.

Maybe you're under-challenged, or overstressed, and you quit your job. Or perhaps, you lose someone you love, or experience a health problem. Life is different now, and you must learn to navigate the unknown.

Maybe you decide to start the novel you've dreamed of writing and other activities become a lower priority. You must make more room in your life for creative expression.

When you find yourself in new territory, you may not feel equipped to handle it. Yes, you need to learn something new, but remember: you bring your deepest values, skills, and abilities—and the choice to change your perspective—with you. And when you need to, you can ground yourself with ritual.

It's time to move beyond your old mindset, and into a new perspective that supports growth. Challenges awaken your dormant abilities. They break the seed open, and from there, you determine whether you will grow.

Joseph Campbell said that we have to let go of the life we planned so we can live the life that is waiting for us. He wasn't telling us not to plan; he was reminding us to listen to our deeper intuition about our purpose. And he was acknowledging the way life unfolds—just when you think you have everything "under control," something can happen to turn your life upside down.

Who Do You Want to Become?

When a change occurs, after the initial shock or realization, our first response is often, "What do I need to do?"

But there is an underlying question that is at the core of the event or realization:

"Who do I need to become to respond creatively to this change?"

It's not just asking what you need to do, it's asking who you need to be to live your creative life. And it's asking what you need to see. Because until you change your viewpoint, you will stay stuck.

Change, especially sudden and unexpected change, challenges your perspective and requires that you grow into a new worldview. You have to build a "new normal," which can take time. Changing your perspective is often a gradual process, requiring faith and practice.

Your perspectives will be challenged, because this path requires growth. During this process, it's helpful to remember these ideas:
- Perspectives are powerful, yet often semi-conscious. They set the direction for, and drive, your life.
- Using curiosity and logic can help you become more conscious of your perspectives, so you can work on changing those that no longer serve you.
- You must choose your new perspective consciously, and take responsibility for that choice.

Your life will be different when you are different in your life.

The Power of Perspective

I believe that not only do we communicate our thoughts to others nonverbally, but our thoughts also have real energy to them. I learned this in a dramatic, direct way when I was nine years old.

My family had just moved to a new town where I knew no one. I was very nervous about going to a new school, especially given my introversion and sensitivity. It was scary to get on the school bus for the first time. I felt everyone's eyes on me as I walked down the aisle to an open seat. What did they think of me? How would they treat me?

I'm sure my doubts and fears showed in my expression, in the way I held myself. I'd also come from a better school system, and was a little bit ahead of everyone else in my grade. I knew most of the answers in class. Unknowingly, I was signaling to the most insecure kids, with the least-developed consciences, that I was the perfect target.

Some kids were mean to me. No one physically attacked me, but they said cruel things. I no longer remember what they said; if I did I would probably roll my eyes at it now. But back then? It hurt.

Every day for the first two weeks of school, I came home after school and cried. I'd tell my mom about it, and a part of me thought she should intervene. Thank goodness she didn't.

One afternoon, as I sat on the floor of my parents' bedroom, telling her what had happened, I thought, or perhaps even said, "There is no way I would *ever* treat another human being that way!"

Something clicked. As soon as I realized I had no respect for those kids, I didn't care what they thought of me.

And then, something interesting happened. The very next day, no one was mean to me—no cruel teasing or attempts to belittle me. It was that dramatic. *Overnight.*

Of course, there were a few times over the years, when a mean kid would say something to try to hurt me, but it didn't get under my skin.

That's probably why it rarely happened.

I learned that there is real energy in our beliefs. Every time I tried not to care, it didn't work. It was only when I really didn't care, that the miracle happened. And it was based on being in alignment with my values.

I didn't try to put on a "tough" skin, or act like someone I wasn't. I stayed true to myself, and learned an important lesson about life. I could be both vulnerable and strong.

It was a huge insight into how we influence others to treat us. It doesn't absolve the mean kids of the responsibility for their actions. But it taught me that I was not a helpless victim; I had my own inner authority, and when I was aligned with it, others respected that.

That is the power of what you think. When you change your perspective, you can change your life.

What You Believe, You Create

In *The Wizard of Oz*, the Scarecrow, the Tin Man, and the Cowardly Lion must confront their respective beliefs that they are not smart, sensitive, or courageous enough.

On the Yellow Brick Road, they discover that they already have these qualities. The situations they encounter bring forth their gifts, and give them the confidence to believe in themselves. It was their previous beliefs that held them back, not their innate abilities.

When you don't think something is possible, you undermine it from the start. Doubt is a destructive force. Hedging on believing in your future does not protect you from disappointment, it just sets you up to fail.

If you feel you are lacking in some quality or experience, remember that the Earth supports a huge variety of life. When you believe in bigger possibilities, you actively co-create those possibilities, using whatever resources you have.

It takes a bigger view to see a new path. Examine your beliefs. Be curious. Go deeper.

Choose a bigger perspective.

You Are Part of the Flow

Your perspective is the way that you look at things. But it's more than just a vantage point; it's a lens that picks up certain details, and ignores others. We all bring preconceived ideas and beliefs into our perspectives, and we draw conclusions from them.

An old Chinese proverb about delaying judgment has helped me stay open about whether situations are "good" or "bad":

> A farmer and his son had a stallion who helped the family earn a living. One day, the horse ran away and their neighbors said, "Your horse ran away, what awful luck!" The farmer kept his equanimity and replied, "The story's not over yet."
>
> A few days later, the horse returned home, leading a few wild mares back to the farm as well. The neighbors said, "Your horse has returned, and brought several horses home with him. What wonderful luck!" The farmer kept his equanimity and replied, "The story's not over yet."
>
> Later that week, the farmer's son was trying to ride one of the mares and she threw him to the ground, breaking his leg. The villagers said, "Your son broke his leg, what horrible luck!" The farmer kept his equanimity and replied, "The story's not over yet."
>
> A few weeks later, soldiers from the national army marched through town, recruiting all the able-bodied boys. They did not take the farmer's son, because his leg was not yet healed. The villagers said, "Your boy is spared, what tremendous luck!" The farmer kept his equanimity and replied, "The story's not over yet."

You get the gist. This story illustrates how life is full of ups and downs. You can choose to react strongly to every event, or look at it from the perspective of the bigger flow.

On the surface, being laid off when I was still recovering from an illness could have appeared to be bad luck. But in reality, it helped save my life.

Exercise: **Discover Your Perspectives**

1. What are some perspectives that you live by?

    For example:

    "It's too hard."
    "I'm in awe."
    "I'm overwhelmed."
    "I'm curious."
    "I'm not good enough."
    "Creativity is abundant."
    "It's too late."
    "I have this well in hand."
    "It's not okay to ask for help."
    "Life is unfolding exactly as it should."
    "Life isn't fair."

2. Which of those perspectives empowers your authority to create your life?

3. Which of those perspectives distracts you from creating your life, by focusing on things you can't control?

4. How do you feel when you're looking at life from a perspective that doesn't support your power and authority to create your life?

    Do you feel calm and clear, or anxious, angry, or depressed?

    How effective are you from that place?

5. When life doesn't go as planned, what would be different if you ask the question, "What can I create from this?"

Perspective Is a Choice

You know your perspective is limiting your consciousness when you're stuck in the same old way of looking at things, and it doesn't support your growth.

As an empathic and "highly sensitive person," I'm taking in a lot of information. If I'm talking with someone, I'm not only listening to their words, I may be intuiting the underlying meaning, feeling their emotional state, smelling odors such as perfume, aftershave, or bad breath, noticing my own body comfort, keenly aware of what I'm feeling, noticing any number of my own thoughts that intrude, aware of movement, sounds, and the emotional states of those around us—and trying to "bottom line" whatever the person is telling me, so I can put it in a meaningful context and understand if I need to do anything, and if so, decide what I need to do.

Whew! That's exhausting. I have to consciously filter out much of that when I'm having deeper conversations.

I'm easily overwhelmed by too much stimuli, including, from my perspective, "too many words."

When I was a teenager, I practically ran from class to class in school. I had to get away from the throng of other kids in the hall, as soon as possible. I'd get to my next class, stake out a seat that "felt" good, and have a few minutes of, if not alone time, at least less-crowded time. It was overwhelming to feel my own deep emotions, as well as all the teenage angst around me.

Over time, "overwhelm" became a comfort zone for me. It felt normal, even though I was uncomfortable. And my coping mechanism—to withdraw from the situation, which served me well as a teenager—stopped serving me. I needed to learn a new way of looking at my life.

Many years later, when I was in a toxic work situation, I tried to tough it out because of another perspective that I'd adopted in college: I had to work at a job that I hated because otherwise, I would starve on the streets. I believed it was the only way to support myself.

I felt powerless.

That's when I began to work with a life coach to help me find a way to move from the landscape of Overwhelm to the territory of Self-Authority.

When my coach gently but firmly suggested that being overwhelmed is a perspective, I balked. My inner teenager responded that I *was* overwhelmed. Look at all the things I had to do! And besides, I'm so sensitive.... You get the picture.

Yes, I'm sensitive, but that doesn't absolve me of being responsible for myself, and for my creative responses to situations.

Now, when I'm feeling overwhelmed, I get curious. I entertain the possibility that I can choose another perspective. Often, I choose the perspective that it is a good practice for me to stay on course when I'm feeling pressure to give up. When I look at commitment from the perspective of spiritual growth, it provides a meaningful context and taps into one of my biggest values: to continue to build spiritual resilience.

Exercise: **Choose Your Perspectives**
1. What perspectives do you overuse?
2. What perspectives do you not use enough?
3. What new perspectives do you want to try going forward?

How Your Perspective Can Help You

Perspective is where experience and the mind meet, informed by the spirit.

You can choose the perspective that the world is magical and beautiful, and you belong here. You can believe that you are meant to grow and experience and expand. You can feel that your life is deeply meaningful, and you have a calling—many callings, in fact.

Why? Because choosing those perspectives allows you to see the connectedness of things, the meaning in events, and the beauty of being here. They support your belief in yourself.

You can choose a dour perspective, if you wish, but all that gets you is staying stuck in the same negative experiences, over and over. It's up to you to choose how you want to live your life.

For example, if you're traveling where you don't know the language, you can't just walk into a store and ask for what you need. You have to stop and think about it, look it up in a phrasebook, speak it phonetically, and hope the sales clerk understands what you mean.

There's a barrier, and to step through it, you have to be willing to be uncomfortable, feel frustrated, or even look ridiculous.

The time I pantomimed cleaning my ears with a cotton swab in a Paris drugstore teased a small smile out of the formal, reserved saleswoman. Only later did I wonder if twirling your finger near your ear was an international gesture for "crazy."

I could have looked at that kind of barrier as a huge problem, one more thing that made international travel more of a chore than fun. But I never did. It was an exciting experience to me, because it was new and it required me to think on my feet, be open, and take risks. And that is the perspective that supports me when I'm trying to make my way through unfamiliar terrain.

Exercise: **Evaluate Your Perspectives**

1. Think of those days when you wake feeling great, when everything in your day clicks, and things feel almost effortless.

   What is it like for you?

2. Now, think of those other days when you wake in a negative cloud, everything feels "off," and nothing seems to work.

   What is that like?

3. And finally, think of those days when your positive mindset helps you navigate the things that go wrong—and also the days when your negative mindset won't let you appreciate how well things are going.

   What do you notice?

   How does your perspective make your experience better or worse?

The Limits of Your Perspective

Perspective is the context of the story you tell yourself about events and situations in your life. When we don't have all the information, our minds fill in the blanks, based on our vantage point. That's why two people can witness the same thing and give not only different, but conflicting accounts.

It's like the metaphor of the blind men trying to describe an elephant, based on touch:

> The first blind man felt its trunk, and said, "An elephant is like a snake."
>
> The second felt its massive leg, and said, "An elephant is like a tree."
>
> The third felt its tail, and said, "An elephant is like a rope."
>
> The fourth felt its ear and said, "The elephant is like a fan."
>
> The next felt the end of the elephant's tusk, and said, "The elephant is like a spear."
>
> The final blind man felt its massive side, and said, "The elephant is like a wall."

Each one was right about the part he touched, but wrong when he tried to describe the elephant as a whole, based on his limited perception.

We do that too, when we take a limiting perspective and blanket our experiences with it.

Our individual perspective is never the complete picture, and yet we base our beliefs and behavior on it. When we absorb negative beliefs, and base our actions on them, they skew the outcome, often becoming a self-fulfilling prophecy.

How to Change Your Perspective

How do you change your perspective?

I had one of my favorite dreams a few years ago, during a time when I felt stuck in a soulless job, and I was working with a life coach to help me move toward more fulfilling work.

I dreamed that a little hedgehog was in a cardboard box and could not get out. I empathized so much with the little creature that it was painful for me to watch it struggling to climb up the sides, only to keep falling back in.

Then, in an *aha!* moment, my dreaming self gently tipped the box onto its side, and the hedgehog walked out, free. I literally changed the perspective, the vantage point.

Changing my perspective seemed so easy in the dream, but it took a lot of time, effort, and support to change my perspective in my waking life. I had to learn to play with reframing my perspectives when they were keeping me stuck. By playing with certain perspectives, I discovered that I could more consciously and creatively direct my free will, rather than react from negative or destructive mindsets.

When you take responsibility for how you view the world, you gain real freedom and mastery over yourself and your experiences.

Reframing is the conscious decision to look at a situation from a different perspective. It's like trying on a new hat. You're trying it on; you haven't decided yet whether it's "you." The mere act of allowing yourself to consider an entirely different perspective opens up new possibilities.

Reframing is not lying to yourself. Pretending to think or feel something that you do not is a form of avoidance, and it doesn't work. All it leads to is cognitive dissonance and, often, a messy personal life. Do it too much and too long, and you become a crazy-making agent in other people's lives.

So, when you decide to look at life from a different a perspective, don't try to force it, just try it on. Wear it for a day, and notice what is different for you.

When you want to reframe how you view a situation, you can move your physical vantage point, adjust the mental lens you're looking through, or change your emotional point of focus.

Moving Your Physical Vantage Point

For me, changing my physical surroundings helps me shift my perspective—even my mood. It shakes things up and gets me out of a rut.

Go Somewhere Different

Changing your location is a quick and easy way to refresh your perspective. I usually go to a local coffee shop or a café that allows me the time and space to write.

Travel is especially helpful. When I traveled to Italy and France while I was working at a "regular" job, I realized how big the world really is, with people making a living doing a myriad of things. Sitting in a cubicle or office, doing work that is not interesting to you, is not the only way to make a life in this world!

Rearrange Things

Changing your environment can be like unblocking a dam in a river. Ever since I was a little girl, I've needed to periodically rearrange my living environment. As a child and teenager, I rearranged my bedroom. Now, I rearrange my living room (and other spaces) when I feel the need for a change.

I can't explain how, but it shifts the energy for me. When I'm feeling stuck, it frees the flow. As I write these words, I'm sitting at the dining room table, which my husband helped me move into the living room of our little house, so I can be surrounded by windows and light. I know it's helped me to finish this chapter.

If you don't want to move furniture around, try changing the decorations on your walls, the knick-knacks on your tables, or painting a wall a new accent color. It can make a big difference.

Adjusting Your Mental Lens

When your mental focus gets stuck—especially in a negative place—adjusting your mental lens can help you shake off the dust and see other possibilities.

Get Curious

One of the fastest ways to get out of a negative perspective that doesn't serve you is to move into curiosity.

When you encounter roadblocks, or resistance in yourself or others, have whatever reaction you're going to have. Then, get curious. Try looking at the situation through new eyes.

What does getting curious do for you?

- It opens you to seeing possibilities that might not occur to you otherwise.
- It moves you out of judgment about the situation—for the time being, at least. Remember, "the story's not over yet."
- It exercises the "muscle" of choosing your perspective.

Curiosity is a lens through which you play with different perspectives and discover insights. I like to think of it as a kitten bounding through the world, exploring and trying new things. Follow your curiosity's lead.

Being curious allows you to be open to possibilities. It suspends your mind's judgment to let your inner guide inform you of the deeper meaning of an event, or of new information. It is supported by the thought, "I wonder."

Curiosity can shift you out of Overwhelm and move you out of a dead-end perspective. Instead of judging yourself or your circumstances, ask questions. Seek to understand something new about the situation. You may be surprised at what shifts for you when you exercise your curious nature.

Get Rational

When I was waiting to speak on stage for the first time about this book, I felt like I was going to die. If it hadn't been so traumatic, it would have been fascinating at the time, because just as I felt so strongly that I would not survive, I knew that I would.

Latching onto the rational thought that I was not literally going to die was the only thing—besides my promise to myself and my coach—that kept me from running down the aisle and out the door.

Rational thought is like dropping a lens in front of your eyes, to block out the emotional "noise" so you can see more clearly.

When you're highly emotional, when something you value is threatened, try to consciously slow your thoughts. Test them against logic to ground them in reality.

For example, when you're afraid you can't do something that is deeply important to you—like your creative practice—and you're afraid it's too late, measure that belief against all the times you have accomplished something, even when you thought you couldn't do it. If you need help, do this with a friend who will provide concrete examples.

Take a deep breath, and channel your inner Spock.

Do Something Completely Different

Having a new experience, like going to a play, a concert, or an art exhibit, gets you out of your ordinary world and seeing with fresh eyes. Try going to a bookstore and browsing the new and recommended books.

Express Your Creativity Through a Different Medium

Doing something creative that isn't my main creative outlet shifts my perspective. I'll take a break from writing and paint. Sometimes, I'll grab the camera and take photos. If no one's around (and sometimes, even when someone is), I'll sing.

Spend Time with Positive People

I can't say this enough: socializing or working with others whose positive viewpoints you share—or want to grow to share—can change your life. My coach always says that your life moves in the direction of the conversations you have the most, and he's right.

Especially if you're highly empathic, you may easily absorb the feelings and moods of those around you. If this is true for you, you must make conscious choices for yourself about who to spend time with, and how much time to spend with them. I know when I am struggling with my own negativity, I am much less able to deal with being around other people's toxic viewpoints.

Changing Your Emotional Focus

Focusing on the good in your life and helping others are effective ways to get clarity about what really matters.

Engage with Someone You Love

When you engage emotionally with someone you love, it gets you out of focusing too much on yourself. Give your spouse a hug, or talk with a friend. Pet your dog, cat, or iguana.

Let someone know how much you love them.

Practice Gratitude

Worry and regret take you out of the present, and keep you spinning in "what if?" One of the quickest ways to reset your perspective spiritually is through practicing gratitude.

Taking the time to notice all the goodness in your life, however small that seems, can help you shift to a more positive place.

Help Someone

Offer to mow the lawn for an elderly neighbor. Help a friend sort through the closet she's been putting off cleaning. Volunteer to walk the dogs at your local animal shelter. Stop focusing on yourself for a while.

You may be surprised how supporting the potential in the lives of others helps you see and believe in your own potential.

It's often just mindset that holds us back.

Exercise: **Practice Switching Lenses**

1. Name the lenses you look through when you're overwhelmed.

    For example, one lens might be "helpless." Another might be "not good enough."

2. What about when you're excited and optimistic?

    One lens might be "people are good," or "the world is beautiful."

3. The next time you feel helpless or not good enough, consciously try to look through another lens.

    If you find this difficult, try just being curious about the situation.

4. Entertain the idea that although you may be right, you may also be missing some key information that could shift your perspective a little.

    Dare to go deeper. You may be surprised at what you learn—and how freeing it is!

Which Perspective Supports Your Authentic Life?

Two foundational life perspectives can either undermine or support you in living your authentic life: viewing yourself as a victim of circumstance, or as a creator. The one you choose sets the course for your life experiences.

Victim of Circumstance

When you're a victim of circumstance, you need help.

If a tornado demolishes your house, you need help. If you are physically attacked, you need help. Identifying yourself as a victim can help you get the support you need.

However, when you identify as a victim in situations where you are able to help yourself, you stay stuck.

When I was in a job that had lost its meaning, yes, I was a "victim" of a deteriorating company culture and an economic recession. For too long, however, I didn't get the help I needed, because I couldn't see a way out. I kept waiting for life to change, rather than taking action to change my life.

I believed I was powerless to change my life, so I stayed stuck.

Creator

When you are a creator, you take what life brings you, and make something new.

After being a victim of circumstance, you choose to rebuild. You leave helplessness, blame, and resentment behind, because they steal from your future.

You know you are already creating your life, all the time; you are a natural creator. Choosing this perspective keeps the power to change your life where it belongs: with you.

When I accepted that my life was not going to change unless I began to invest in my own growth, I looked at life from the perspective of a creator. I hired a life coach, and began creating this path.

It has made all the difference in the world.

Exercise: **Compare Victim and Creator Perspectives**
1. Think of a situation where you felt like a victim of your circumstances.
   What was the cost of that perspective?
   What was the benefit?
2. Think of a situation where you took responsibility for changing your circumstances.
   What was the cost of that perspective?
   What was the benefit?

Five Secrets of Living a Creative Life

Use these five perspectives to guide you as you blaze your creative path. Through practice, they will help you make positive choices.

What you believe, you create. Your beliefs create the trajectory of your life. Your freedom lies in choosing your perspective. Choosing perspectives that support your spirit will change your life.

You are creating all the time—in your life, and of your life. You are always in the creative flow. Even when the stream goes underground, your spirit is doing deep work, transforming your experiences so that you can bring them into the light.

Life brings you the material to co-create your art and the life you want. The universe is not an inert void where you are meant to scratch out a miserable existence; it is inherently and abundantly creative; it responds to you.

When you respond creatively, your creative power expands. Life challenges you to respond, rather than simply react. Trying to control everything in your life saps your creative power; responding creatively channels your power.

As you create your art, your art shapes you. As you respond creatively, and as you make art from your experiences, you become who you need to be to write your next story, paint your next masterpiece, sing your next song—and create your best life.

Dancing with the Muse

"Start a huge, foolish project, like Noah. It makes absolutely no difference what people think of you."
Rumi

When I lost my job, I knew I could not go back to the same career. Luckily, I had already invested in myself by completing life-coach training, and beginning the rigorous certification process. I had a direction—coaching—and a passion—writing—and a big, blank canvas to make a new life.

I didn't know what to do first.

I knew how to coach, but I didn't know how to be an entrepreneur.

I knew how to write. But what did I want to write about?

I had the beginning of a novel and some short stories that needed work. But I wasn't pulled to focus on them. Instead, I needed to write as a way to find myself again. I started a weekly blog.

Each week, the thread of an idea wove itself with words into something I wanted to say—and I didn't always know what direction it would take.

Each week, I danced with the muse by taking imperfect action. By writing messy first drafts that slowly began to take form.

I moved from chaos to inspiration.

CHAPTER 8

Creativity Is Messy

You should have seen this page as I was writing earlier drafts of this book. There were scribbled-out words, notes to move content from another part of the book to here, arrows, and new paragraphs written in sparkly teal ink in the margins.

It was a mess while I developed my ideas. Slowly, it took its initial form. The chaos was daunting. The developing form was inspiring. I just had to stick with it and allow the muse to show up and take me in the direction I needed to go.

I love how scientists are using infrared scanning and multi-spectral imaging technology to look beneath masterpieces to find images that artists painted over. There's a man in a bow tie beneath Picasso's *The Blue Room*. How cool is that?

Creative expression is full of false starts and changes in direction. It's a fluid, not linear, process—and that's what makes it so fun and interesting.

CHAPTER 9

Trusting the Potential in Chaos

How do you discover the potential in chaos? You play.

If you're like me, your first response to an insight or inspiring new idea is to jump on your horse and ride madly off in all directions, metaphorically speaking.

Why? Because you're excited! You see all the possibilities and want to get started as soon as possible! (I bet you couldn't even stop yourself from overusing exclamation points!!!)

And for a period of time, this is exactly what you need to do.

This phase is not about forming and executing a "perfect" plan. It's about shaking things up, to wake yourself up, to keep yourself awake and aware.

When a new idea, or a piece of art is preparing to come into the world through you, there's chaos. Lots of ideas, emotions, and insights swirl around in your consciousness.

Trying to pin these down too soon clips the wings of your expression, when it needs to fly.

Let it be.

When it's ready, it will alight in your mind. You will see it clearly.

Have faith in the process. You can't know what the outcome will be. Focus on the journey—on getting there—and trust that you're on a path that supports your growth.

Trust moves you through the barriers of negative thinking, letting you see what is possible, and allowing the universe to co-create your life and art. It helps you let go of attachment to how something will happen, which can bog you down in why things can't or won't work. When you have faith, miracles can happen.

Intuition is the whisper of your inner sage, guiding you. It is like a subtle movement in the trees, or the soft sound of a pebble dropping to the ground.

When you listen to your inner wisdom, you find imaginative routes that are rich with possibility. Pay attention to messages that come to you, in books that fall open to a certain page, or in the lyrics of a song on the radio. Allow moments of synchronicity to lead you in unexpected directions. If you feel pulled to do something, do it.

Play and Experiment

Revel in the chaos of newness. Do anything creative that feels fun and inspiring. Take your first steps. Let one thing lead to another.

Follow the path in front of you.

How can you begin to bring more creativity into your daily life? Start small, and build on that. But do it every day.

Spend at least 15 minutes every day playing and experimenting with your creative expression.

If you're a painter, then paint. Have fun! Work on a design, or just play with color. Do whatever you feel moved to do, not what you think you "should" do. If the allocated time passes and you want to keep going, keep going.

Leave the dishes for later.

If you're a writer, then write. Block out the world and begin.

If you're feeling uninspired, take three words—like orange, airplane, and briefcase—and write a description or a vignette that uses each of those words at least once.

Or just write about how you're feeling in the moment.

Make a collage. Sing. Write a poem.
Go for a walk and daydream.
You can always run the vacuum cleaner tomorrow.

CHAPTER 10

Tapping into Inspiration

Creativity is the energy of life and growth. It takes potential, and makes it real. A tree from an acorn, a baby from a fertilized egg—that is creation in the natural world.

Just go for a walk, and you see: creative energy is abundant. It flows through the grass and leaves, the soil, the air and clouds, the water. You can feel it! It flows through everything, like invisible radio waves.

Maya Angelou said that we can't use up creativity; the more we use, the more we have. She was right.

How do you tap into the creative energy that is available to you? Through the inspiration of the muse.

It's time to dance!

Go with an impulse that came out of chaos. Pick a direction and begin in earnest. Allow yourself to take imperfect action. Explore and discover, play and make mistakes. Follow clues and have fun.

You have to start somewhere!

Who Is the Muse?

The muse is the archetypal personification of artistic inspiration. In Greek mythology, the Muses were the goddesses who inspired literature, science, and the arts.

Creative energy flows through everything, including us. I think of the muse as the conduit for that crackling energy, communicating to us through flashes of intuition and inspiration. Then, we act as a lens through which that inspiration is focused into our unique creative expressions.

This is similar to Elizabeth Gilbert's belief that ideas are floating around looking for a home, and our muse is the doorway to receiving those ideas.

I was lucky to hear Gilbert speak at the first Emerging Women's Conference in Boulder, Colorado. She talked about beginning to write a book, and sending a synopsis to her publisher. As she began to describe the book, I realized that I had just read that book, by another author. It was Ann Patchett's *State of Wonder*.

As I listened to Gilbert, an electric excitement pulsed through me. I could see the non-rational structure of reality, the mysterious way the world works that defies logical explanation. Because I had just read Patchett's book, I knew what Gilbert was going to say: that ideas have a life of their own. Each potential is waiting for someone to make it real, and sometimes, more than one person picks up on it.

How does that happen?

I know that we are all connected. I have had detailed dreams that happened in waking life the next day—sometimes about the most mundane things, involving people I know but am not in regular contact with. When Gilbert told the story, I wondered whether she is so empathically and psychically tuned that she picked up on Patchett's idea.

But I also like Gilbert's belief that inspiration is out there waiting to land somewhere. However it happens, it reminds me that the everyday is actually miraculous.

Anything that inspires you can be your muse, calling you to dance in the creative moment. Other writers and artists can serve as muses, transferring the electricity of inspiration to you.

If you make yourself available, as the instrument and the musician, inspiration flows through you and into your creations.

Exercise: **Know Your Muse**
1. Who are some artists who serve as muses for you?
2. Imagine you have a personal muse.
   This is the voice that whispers in your ear when you're trying to sleep, and you have to get up and capture what she says.
3. Name your muse—don't think about it!
4. What are the qualities you associate with your muse?
5. What inspires you about those qualities?

How Does It Feel to Dance with Your Muse?

Dancing is about timing, rhythm, and movement—taking steps to the music you hear.

When you dance with your muse, you're connected to creative energy. It flows through you. Your feet don't quite touch the ground, and you're twirling in a current of feeling, intuition, and ideas.

When you're in the creative flow, it feels magical, as though you're channeling words, or brush strokes, from your muse.

You might experience fortuitous synchronicities, clues that you're on the right path.

When your muse calls to you, you have a choice. You can grasp her extended hand and join her. Or you can put her off, and tell her that you'll dance later.

Sometimes, you can jump back in the dance where you left off. But often, the moment is lost.

Imagine you are in a ballroom, filled with light. Someone extends a hand to you, saying, "Would you like to dance?"

And you reply, "Yes, after I clean the house."

Really?

Then you leave to run errands and check things off your to-do list, including the house cleaning.

When you run back to the dance, breathless, you find the lights are out, the music has faded, the ballroom door is locked, and your muse is gone.

Your creativity is not here to serve you.

You are not here to serve your creativity.

When you create, something simply wants to be born.

The muse is your dance partner in creation. When she calls, treat her with respect. Give her your attention. Listen to her. Nourish and nurture her.

Take steps when she whispers in your ear.

Here is an example of how I experienced dancing with the muse.

A friend posted Amedeo Modigliani's *Portrait de Jeanne Hébuterne* on Facebook, with the question, "What is she thinking?"

Although Modigliani painted his wife's portrait in 1919, I felt that I was looking at a woman painted in the 1950s.

I found myself writing this:

> She's remembering dancing last night at the Elks Club with Hugo, the town grocer, how he twirled her like a ballerina and smelled of cardboard boxes and spicy aftershave.
>
> He noticed she was wearing two different earrings—a fox and a bird—and said, "A fox is clever, and a bird sees everything."

> *She felt his hazel eyes looked into her very soul. He saw and appreciated the eccentricities her family mocked—like how she only wrote with purple ink, and how she mixed the details of whatever books she was reading, so that they clung together, forever altered, dangling on the Christmas tree of her mind.*
>
> *She wants to go to the grocery just to see him. To test if what she felt the night before was real, or whether the light of a regular day will swallow the magic of their connection, like a stone dropped into a dark, still pool.*

I was inspired, just from looking at a painting and considering the question, "What is she thinking?"

At first, I was tempted to reply with something tongue-in-cheek, like "She's wondering if she left the stove on."

But my muse got my attention. There was something deeper that wanted to be expressed. I felt like the woman in the painting had a story, and she wanted me to tell it.

So instead of doing what I had planned to do with my Sunday morning, I sat in my comfy chair and wrote until I felt I had said what wanted to be said.

When my muse asked me to dance, I said "Yes."

Exercise: **Respond to Your Muse**
1. Describe a time when the muse asked you to dance, and you said "Yes."
   What did you do?
   What was it like?
2. Describe a time when your muse asked you to dance, but you put her off, or said "No."
   Was it easy to tap into her inspiration later, when you wanted to?
   If yes, why do you think that was?
   If no, why not?

How to Invite Your Muse

To create, to better hear the whispers of your muse, you need to invite her by making time and space for her.

Uninterrupted Time

I keep relearning what I already know, again and again.

As I write this, I just lost patience with my best friend, my husband and partner—because I wasn't clear with him about what I really need to finish this book. It is perfect that this happened, because it is a good example of the concept I need to address here, at a deeper level.

In addition to being a writer and painter, I am a business owner. I need to make or be involved in business decisions every day, but I do my best creative work in the morning. I believe it has something to do with the light and the proximity to the unconsciousness of sleep. And if I am interrupted—by general chitchat, strategy discussions, or business details—I lose the flow, and I have trouble getting it back.

I need a block of uninterrupted time in the morning to do my creative work. But I was inadvertently giving my partner mixed signals, by leaving my office to sit out in our shared space, have breakfast, and watch a little zone-out TV, which gives me a short break halfway through the morning.

Although I appear to be available—for questions or to pass along information—I'm really not.

Here's what I keep relearning: my creative time is sacred. Those little moments talking with my husband are precious to me. Our business discussions are essential for success. But not when I'm writing.

Yet, I hear a little, inner voice that tells me I'm being "unreasonable" if I'm not available to my partner when he has a question or needs to communicate something. Especially when my husband and best friend just wants to connect with me.

As someone wise once said, "It's not mean to state a fact."

In fact, it's much less kind to quietly stew as my boundaries are being crossed, and say nothing, until I finally lose patience. It's not fair to the other person, and it's a complete waste of emotional energy for me.

So instead of impatiently "listening" to my partner when I'm writing or taking a needed break, I could have simply told him what I needed, and—just as importantly—modeled that behavior. By respecting those boundaries myself, such as declining invitations that intrude upon my creative time and sticking to my schedule, I demonstrate my commitment.

This is your life. Only you can claim what you need to create.

Habits either support or undermine your dreams. If you want to write a story, you must write on a regular basis. If your habit of checking email undermines your writing, disconnect.

Build creativity into your schedule by blocking out time for your creative expression.

Exercise: **Claim Your Creative Space**

1. What do you need to meet your creative needs (boundaries, communication)?
2. What do you need to do your creative work (materials, space, time)?
3. How much time do you really have for your creative practice?

    To determine the free time you have each week, subtract the time you spend doing the activities below from the total number of hours in a week:

Total number of hours in a week:	168
Working/commuting	-
Spending time with your family	-
Doing housework	-
Cooking/eating	-
Exercising	-
Participating in leisure activities	-
Sleeping	-
Other	-
TOTAL free hours per week	=

4. How can you claim what you need to create?

A Room of Your Own

Virginia Woolf was right: you must have a room of your own—to write, to paint, to create, to be.

When everything is new, you need to give the chaos of creativity some structure and boundaries to blossom within. Like a fertile pot of soil.

If you don't have a room of your own, it's time to claim it.

A room of your own is a dedicated space that is exclusively yours. It is not a room doing double duty.

When I think about double-duty creative spaces, I'm reminded of a skit from the *Saturday Night Live* comedy TV show, in which Gilda Radner—with her lovable, goofy grin—declared: "It's a floor wax, *and* a dessert topping!"

Is it a painting studio, or a workout room? Is it a place to write, or a guest room? Is it your sanctuary, or the junk room?

You need to pick one.

You must have a space free of distractions, that is all your own, to support your calling. If you do other things in that room—or other people use that room—it's not exclusive space.

Caveat: If your creative space must do double duty, create visible boundaries around your creative area. Put up a screen to get the exercise machine, guest bed, or boxes out of your sight when you're creating. Decorate the screen to make it feel like your space.

And finally, if you do not have space you can claim in your home, try your local library or favorite coffeehouse. Even though I have dedicated creative spaces, I often get out of the house so I'm not tempted to do chores or spoil my darling dog!

Get Rid of Clutter

Closets stuffed with clothes, handbags, and shoes you haven't worn in years.

Junk drawers filled with expired batteries, rubber bands, and dried-up pens. Half the time when you try to open these drawers, they get stuck!

Bookshelves crammed with books behind piles of more books. Some are favorites, others you've read but will never read again, and more you haven't read but think you'll read "someday."

Boxes filled with your children's drawings, letters from your grandmother, cards from your spouse, parents, and dear friends. Old toys, knick-knacks, and bank statements from decades ago.

There is an emotional weight to accumulated things.

There is a cost to having too much stuff.

Honoring your creative space is essential to supporting your creative work, whatever it may be.

When things clutter your living and working areas, they also take up space in your mind and heart. Getting rid of stuff you don't need or want makes room for what you do need and want. It gives you the space and perspective to see a new possibility: room to breathe.

Yes, chaos fertilizes the soil of creativity, but too much outer chaos can confuse rather than inspire. Clutter is like a visual, failed-to-do list. It not only shows you what you need to do, it reminds you of what you haven't done. I don't know about you, but my inner dragon has a field day with that; it chastises me about how far behind I am.

To be sure, everyone's version of chaos is a little different. Adjust your space to fit you, by listening to how you feel when you're in it. Does it feel mentally spacious? Can you start a project and leave it out while you finish it?

I keep my living spaces mostly free of clutter, and I love how they feel. But over the long period of time before I began to reclaim my creative life, my office and spare room had become nothing more than storage areas. Even though I didn't use those rooms much, the way I felt when I walked by, or went in to get something, weighed on me.

I look at my living space as a kind of mirror of my inner space. My creative space (my office) and my health space (room with the elliptical machine) were completely neglected. Guess which areas of my life I was not honoring?

And truthfully, the neglected rooms/parts of myself got that way during a very difficult time in my life, when it was all I could do to get the basics taken care of. My divorce, the loss of a family member, the death of my dog, a toxic work situation, the lack of any substantive emotional support—all I had to do was look into those rooms to feel the overwhelming grief of those times. The clutter had to go.

Don't get me wrong; some messes are wonderful. It's not about living in a Pottery Barn ad! (Unless you want to.)

I love the way my table looks when I've been painting, with paper and watercolors and a muddy glass of water from rinsing paint out of my brushes. But when I'm finished and I put it all away, it clears space for my next creative project.

The messes left over from fun, creative moments are beautiful in their own way. But the mess left over from putting everything else in my life ahead of my own body and spirit? Not so much.

Go easy on yourself.

Because of the emotional weight of clutter, it can be very difficult to face and tackle on your own. If you let go of shame and embarrassment, treat yourself with compassion—you're not the only person in the world with clutter—and nurture yourself by getting the support you need, you can declutter and open up the parts of your life you've been neglecting.

I hired a professional organizer to help me, and it made a world of difference. She came once a week, and helped me clear space and organize.

Going through my clothes, books, papers, and mementos was difficult. I faced lost dreams, evaluated what I really wanted and what felt like a burden, and learned to let go of what no longer served me.

It was a spiritual process as much as a physical one. The vision of how my living space and my life would feel when it was done kept me motivated.

Ask a friend to help you or hire someone. Whatever you need to do, reclaim your space.

Exercise: **Declutter Your Space**
1. How would discarding things you no longer want or need improve the space you live in?
2. How would that support your creativity?
3. What is holding you back?
4. What do you need to get started?
5. When will you start?

Decorate

If you're like me, the aesthetics of your physical space are hugely important. For me, it needs to feel inviting and beautiful.

In my office, I have some of my own paintings hung on the walls, along with paintings by my great-grandmother, my grandmother, my brother, and my nephew.

On my desk (and shelves above) are flowering plants, my happiness jar, a fairy door, candles, flowers, fountain pens, paintbrushes, and puppy photos of two of my beloved dogs.

Find decorations that inspire you and make you happy in your space. Make it a place where you truly feel free to create and play.

Have fun with it!

Responding to Your Calling

"What you seek is seeking you."
Rumi

When I left the corporate world, I was clear about my callings. I have always been called to write fiction and non-fiction, to paint when the spirit moves me, and to support others in their creative dreams.

Simple, right? Yes and no.

The territory between hearing my calling and answering it was like a wide plain dotted with boulders and hidden chasms. And in the distance, I could see the forest and the sea—the dark, deep places I knew I would enter after I truly committed.

Answering my callings has been a process to reclaim my inner authority—and my outer responsibility. I had to learn to believe in myself again, that I had the right to create a life that aligned with who I was. And I had to grow to make it happen.

After being in limbo for so long, telling myself that I would get to it tomorrow, when my ship came in, when I retired, "someday"—that day in the future became "now."

CHAPTER 11

Creativity Is Spiritual

I believe that creativity is a way to align with our core selves. Being present in a regular, creative practice helps you tap into your wisdom. It's a kind of ultra-focused perspective that allows you to turn inward, and listen to that whispering voice trying to get your attention.

When you couple that with the larger perspective of knowing that you are part of something bigger than yourself, you tap into your true strength.

Whatever you long for and whatever you are pulled to do exists inside of you, wanting to be brought into this world. You recognize it, because when something touches you deeply, it feels like your spirit's echo answering back to you. Your soul has called out; this is the reply.

I think of the unmanifest world as a great, sea-like universe that touches ours. It's hidden, but it's also right here.

When you try to see it, it hides in your peripheral vision. Like the Tao that cannot be named, its existence can only be intuited. Which is why your best ideas often come just as you're waking, or while walking the dog or taking a shower. When you're not trying to focus on the hidden world, the relaxation of your conscious mind allows you to see through the veil.

If your consciousness swims in a sea of possibilities, your creativity is the channel between the unmanifest world of ideas and the world we live in. It allows you to reach through the veil between the two worlds and bring something forth—a poem, a photograph, a painting.

These ideas call to you. When they resonate deeply, you dip your fingers into the sea of possibilities and bring them forth. You give them life, just as you have been given life.

CHAPTER 12

What Is Your Calling?

Your calling is your wake-up call—to awaken to a deep, soulful reason you are here. It is sacred. It leads you to a deeper knowing of yourself, of others, and of this world.

Your calling may be a longing, an impulse, or a lifelong dream.

A wake-up call is especially poignant at midlife, because you've experienced real losses and narrowed choices, and the clock is ticking. You have a sense of urgency.

In its biggest sense, your calling is about service, directly or indirectly. It is what you came here for. It's not a simple path, or even sometimes rational. It is so deep you may only hear its whisper when your mind is quiet. It is delicate and strong. It is what your soul knows, but you may have forgotten.

Don't let the word "calling" psych you out. Your calling isn't necessarily your life's purpose, although it could be.

And you don't have to have One Big Calling, although you can. Most likely, you'll have multiple callings in your lifetime—or even more than one calling at the same time.

We have multiple callings because we are multi-dimensional. You might have a calling to be a parent. And to play the bass. And to write. Those calls may be louder at different times in your life.

Writing this book was a calling. Painting a picture, writing a poem, and sewing a quilt are all callings.

Don't sweat it.

You don't have to make the "right" choice and stick with it forever. You just need to make a choice. Take your first steps, and see where they lead.

You may change or adjust that choice a few times, as you walk the Creative Heroine's Path.

To help identify your calling, begin with what you're passionate about.

Your Passion

Passion is all about aliveness. When you feel so alive and focused that you lose track of time, you are engaged at a passionate level.

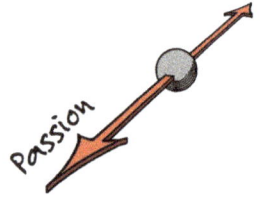

When you can't wait to do something, you are engaged at a passionate level.

When you don't want to stop doing something, you are passionately engaged.

When I am deep into my writing and have to stop, it's actually painful. I resent intrusion—anything else is unimportant.

What fills you with excitement? What makes you come alive?

What, when you're *not* doing it, makes your life feel duller and uninspired?

This is a passion of yours!

Exercise: **Find Your Passion**

These questions are designed to help you get out of your logical, self-critical mind, and go deeper into your intuitive knowing about yourself. Each question is meant to peel back another layer.

Spend some time and go deep. Find a time and a place where you will not be interrupted, and let your wise inner voice take you on a journey.

1. When do you feel the most alive?

    What are you doing?

    Where are you?

    Who are you with?

2. Why do you feel so alive when you are doing that?

    When you are in that place?

    When you are with that person or group?

3. Who are you when you are doing that?

    When you are in that place?

    When you are with that person or group?

4. What do you need more of in your daily life?

5. What wakes you up in the middle of the night with the ache of regret because you're not doing it?

6. What must you not leave this world without doing?

7. Read through all your answers to these questions.

    Now describe your passion—or passions!

Your Purpose

Purpose is not the same as passion. Your passion—your aliveness—is about you. Your purpose is about what you give to others.

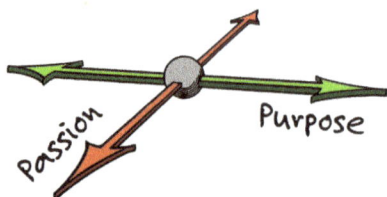

For me, supporting others on their authentic paths has always been a huge part of my life—long before I became a manager or a coach. I think that's because my own life purpose is to grow and become more conscious; I want to support others who are doing the same thing.

In this context, my purpose is to inspire others.

Your purpose is the context for your talents and skills—your gifts—whether you are making a painting, writing a story, coaching a client, or building a business.

All your life, certain things have come so naturally to you that you probably undervalue them. (That doesn't mean you don't put effort into them.) What feels as natural to you as breathing?

Exercise: **Find Your Purpose**

Think of this as a scavenger hunt in your unconscious.

1. Find something you've done naturally, your whole life.

   What comes so easily to you that you often undervalue it?
2. Find something others have always appreciated about you.

   What have many people in your life always wanted from you?
3. Find one of your deeply held beliefs.

   What is a core belief that feels as much a part of you as your very bones?

   Why does it matter so much to you?
4. Find something you secretly have always known about yourself.

   What magic do you possess?
5. Find one thing you've always wanted to do to make the world a better place.

   If you had a magic wand, what would you fix?
6. Read through this list of your treasures.
7. Based on this unique mix, what would you say your purpose is?
8. What is meant to exist in this world, just because of you?

Your Power

Power crackles at the intersection of aliveness and meaning. When your passion and purpose combine, they bring real momentum to your efforts.

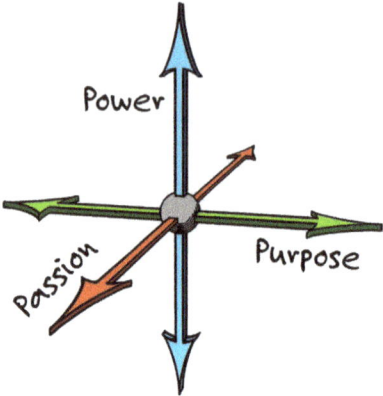

Your power is how you influence, how you make things happen. It is deeply grounded in who you are, and energetically points you to your calling.

You need that power, because answering your calling challenges you at times. Resistance, distraction, and doubt interject, even though you're doing what you love. The power in your passion and purpose helps you keep going.

For me, combining my writing with inspiring and supporting others led me to write a blog, which helped me develop my path and my voice. The power was real; I saw that I could make a difference.

Exercise: **Find Your Power**
1. When have you felt most alive and aligned with your natural abilities?
2. What were you doing?
3. Who were you with?
4. When are you most powerful?

What Is Calling You?

Based on your passion, purpose, and power, what is calling to you now?

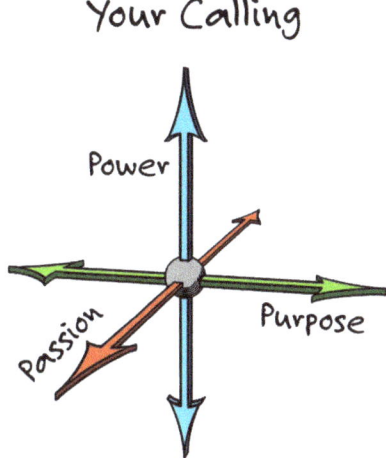

One of my callings was to write this book. I combined my passion—writing—with my purpose—inspiring and supporting others. There are many ways I can combine my passion for writing with my purpose to inspire others. Writing this book was just one calling.

Something wants to come into this world through you, too.

You know your calling is real when you feel the power of alignment. It fills you with energy and meaning. It is the why and how of your passion and purpose.

When passion and purpose intersect, the way shows itself. You may hear it as a whisper, at first, but pay attention.

What is calling you?

What wants to be created in your world?

If Your Calling Is Not Clear to You

If you're struggling to find your calling, don't overthink it. Instead, pay attention to what your spirit responds to. Follow your impulses; they're clues, crumbs left by your soul along the path for you to follow.

When I'm writing a story, sometimes I'll get pulled off onto a tangent. Then, the energy fades and the tangent peters out. Other times, my energy picks up and I follow the change in the path for a long way. I may decide not to use it in the final version, but *I follow the energy.*

If nothing comes, just start something! Waiting until the clouds part and a chorus of angels descends to give you the answer won't work.

Take imperfect action. Go in one direction, and be open to clues. Being leads to doing, and doing leads to becoming. *Do something.*

Act from your power and see what sticks. You are in the process of becoming all your life. You will become who you need to be. Trust that.

Remember:
- Your callings keep showing up, wanting to be expressed through you.
- You know it's your calling when you need to grow into the artist and person you need to be to complete it.
- You know it's your calling when you can't *not* do it and feel fulfilled in this life.

Responding to Your Calling

Exercise: **Find Your Calling**

Your spirit has the intuitive wisdom to show you what is at the intersection of your passion and your purpose.

1. In the following figure, write your *passion* along the red line. Write your *purpose* along the green line.

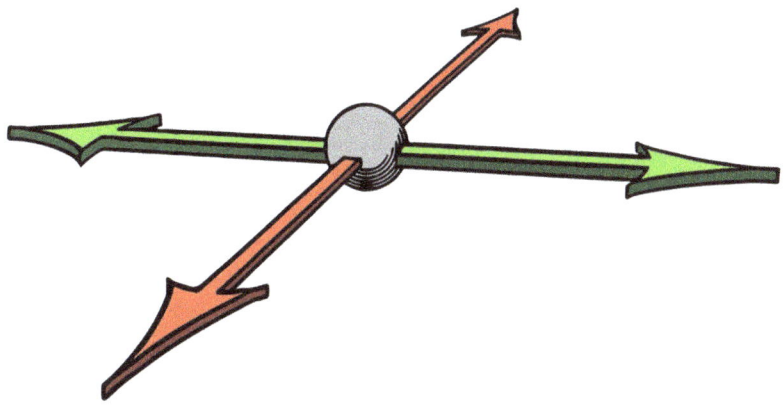

Your positive, natural power forms where your passion and purpose meet.

2. What do you see at the intersection of your passion and your purpose?

    More importantly, what do you feel?

3. What is your intuition whispering to you right now about your calling?
4. What are you called to do now on your life's path?
5. Write what is calling you at the top of the figure.
6. What is one real step you can take this week to begin acting on your calling?
7. Take that step.

    It may lead you somewhere else. It doesn't matter.

    Just start!

CHAPTER 13

Moving from Commitment to Devotion

You're probably better at commitment than I am. I resist it, because it feels like I'm shutting out other possibilities, which of course I am. There comes a point where I must choose one thing over the many others, or I won't do any of them.

I also despise routine, at times.

How, you may be wondering, did I ever finish this book?

First, I made the commitment to keep going, even when I didn't feel like it. Some days I got a lot written; others, not so much.

But because I kept going, something shifted. The original sparks of inspiration ignited into a slow burn of intention and follow-through. I began to feel devoted to this book. It became something real that I cared about, more than an idea, more than a goal.

When you're devoted, your commitment expands with your heart. Even when it's difficult, it's filled with meaning for you. It helps you keep going in hard times.

When you commit to your dream, you answer the call. Devotion is when the meaning of your calling takes root.

This is a pivotal point on your path: will you answer the call? Will you commit to your calling?

Whether you believe your soul moves on to another realm, or is reincarnated back into this world, or that your consciousness dies with your body, your time living this life is limited. That brings a poignant urgency to authenticity and growth.

Don't "what if" your calling.

My most painful dark nights of the soul are regrets about things I wanted to do, but did not. I follow the thorny, well-worn path in my mind of "What if?"

There comes a point on your journey where there is no going back. This is where you make it real.

There are no guarantees, except that one day this life will end. It matters immensely how you choose to live the life that you have left on this beautiful Earth.

Are Your "Shoulds" Sabotaging You?

Creative people are gifted rebels. We see things differently and we do things in our own way. This gets us into trouble, thank goodness! What's life, if it's just living the status quo? It's not enough for us.

You may be a quiet rebel, living your truth without making a lot of waves. Or you may be shouting who you are from the rooftops.

Sometimes, when you make your own to-do lists and tell yourself you "should" do something, guess what? Your inner kindergartener says, "You're not the boss of me."

Why? Because it feels more like a chore than your deep, inspired passion.

So, you procrastinate. Or distract yourself. Or mope. You feed your inner critic bonbons. And you don't finish what you actually want to complete.

Don't get me wrong. I know you're not a slacker. In fact, you are probably super responsible to *other people*. But perhaps not always to yourself.

It hurts when you let yourself down. It can undermine your confidence, sap your enthusiasm, and seduce you into giving up.

I need to ask you something.

Why do you value what you want to do?

Stop.

Don't read any more of this book until you answer that.

Chances are, something came to mind pretty quickly, like "Because I love to paint," or, "I want to make a difference in the world." You might be sitting up a little taller, your backbone straight and strong when you say this.

Now, take that answer and go a little deeper. Ask yourself why this is important to you.

It could be that you feel more alive when you brush paint across a canvas. It could be that you want to make a difference because you care deeply about people. Do you feel a softening in your chest? Are you a little teary-eyed? Are you feeling a little more vulnerable? If so, you're getting closer.

That beautiful combination of strength and vulnerability is telling you something. The value and importance of why you want to create are your energetic roots, and your inner wisdom. Tap into them. Let them ground you and nourish your enthusiasm.

What can you do with all that strength and enthusiasm? You can commit to anything that moves you in the direction of your goal.

You can commit to painting or writing an hour a day. Or playing the piano. Or knitting. Or designing your next piece of jewelry.

Yes, you can.

Ultimately, you have to make that choice. No one else can make you commit. There's no magic potion, spell, or list of steps that will do it. It's up to you.

We don't always know why we finally choose to commit or when it's going to happen. It can be an accumulation of imperceptible inner changes, like an underground stream that travels a long time until it emerges into the light. Or it can be a swift response to an idea or situation, like flipping a switch.

You must make that choice, and act on it. You can do this! I know you can.

If you're hedging, here's a tip: commit to doing something that is a stretch, but not too much. You want it to be doable but not too easy. Why?

You need to make your goal realistic so you can experience success, obviously. But you also need to make sure your goal stretches you, at least a little. Pushing yourself just beyond your comfort zone is more exciting than playing small. And it does three things:

- It moves you further along.
- It teaches you that you can do more than you realized.
- It expands your comfort zone.

Once you experience success, you're even more ready to take the next step and make it meaningful. (And your inner kindergartener loves to get those gold stars!)

Honor your commitment to yourself by taking action. A commitment you make to yourself is just as sacred as a commitment you make to your spouse, or child, or friend.

You'll see how much you can do, and how far you can go, one commitment at a time!

Making It Real

Here's the thing: you have to start, sometimes even before you believe you can do it.

When you are sure you can't do it—and there will be times you'll be certain that's the "truth"—do it anyway. If you focus on your failures and ignore the bigger context and arc of your life, you'll give up, over and over again.

You need champions. Others who see your vision, and believe in it and in you enough to be your Greek chorus of support. Because you have inner dragons and old mindsets that hold you back.

I have a confession to make. If we're looking at this through the Myers-Briggs lens, I'm not big on structure and completion. I like my daily life open-ended. I secretly envy the opposite trait—people who are good at completion. They get so much done!

But I'm easily distract—"Look! A squirrel!"—ed. It's like I've always got my feelers out, taking in information. My intuition and empathy make it so that being around people or animals I am connected to can make it difficult to concentrate.

I used to mentally beat myself up over this. Now, I accept that although I've developed more discipline over the years, my artistic nature is open-ended and non-linear.

The truth is, I needed a deadline to get this book finished. Do whatever you need to do for accountability. Set a deadline with someone who cares—and will check in with you if she hasn't heard a progress report from you in a while.

The Second Wind

The funny thing about writing about discipline is how much I resisted it. In fact, I put a placeholder with the note: "Write about discipline" in a draft of this section.

Then I checked email and Facebook, got a glass of water, and thought about some straightening I need to do in my office.

"I'll just put those things away first." Uh-huh.

For years, I believed that discipline cramped my creative style. And it can: if I don't watch it, I can make the shift from "sticking with it" to Type A energy and linear thinking.

But really, that's just a story, and ironically, it requires discipline to stay in the flow rather than switching to "check it off the list" thinking.

If you're a writer, discipline around your creative practice really means sitting down in your chair and keeping the pen moving on the page, even when you start to get uncomfortable about where you have to go emotionally to write, or when you feel the flow slowing down.

In fact, it's really about getting into the zone and staying with it until you catch a second wind of inspiration.

So, if it helps you (and it helps me) to think of discipline as staying in the creative process until you get that second wind, by all means, think of it that way.

And if it helps you to think of discipline as making a promise to yourself to get back to the page or the canvas or the guitar at a certain time—and keeping that promise—use that too.

Because without discipline, you won't get things done. And your gifts are too precious to let yourself down like that.

Refusing the Call

For a long, long time, I refused the call. Or I answered, but hung up, over and over—every time it got difficult. I wanted some kind of guarantee. But commitment never works as long as you have a "show me" attitude, whether that's in relationships or other parts of life.

I dabbled, keeping the spark of creativity alive, which counts for something. It counts for a lot. But here's my version of refusing the call.

- Take classes on writing, but don't allow myself to be vulnerable enough to write the hard stuff.
- Allow a draconian vacation policy at a salaried job to dictate my traveling life.
- Paint only when I give myself permission to play.

It was like swinging on a trapeze, knowing I had to let go and grab the life that was reaching out to me. But I was afraid.

Everyone has a purpose. To live your purposeful life, you have to take risks. You have to answer the call. Because the voice will never go away; the voice is you. Your inner self knows what you're here for. It is the thread that connects you with the deepest meaning and mysteries of your life.

What does it look like when you aren't answering the call?

Denial—You deny that the call matters, that you can do it, or that you even have a calling.

Putting it on hold—You procrastinate and distract yourself. You always put other things first.

Compromising—"I can't be a creative writer. I'll take classes in technical writing. At least I'll be using some of my skills."

What if you choose not to answer the call?

There's no shame in not answering it. I actually worked with my first life coach for a short time before I re-hired her a few years later and began working in earnest.

Why? Because the first time I worked with her, I knew I had to make life changes that I wasn't ready to make yet. I reconnected with her only when the pain of not changing was worse than the growth and changes required of me.

If you don't answer the call, you may simply not be ready yet.

But I hope you do answer the call, because the world needs your gifts.

The Cost of Refusing the Call

When I was a freshman in college, I was bored. I was attending a local university, taking general classes, some of them in theater-like rooms with hundreds of other students. One class challenged me so little that I rarely needed to attend; all I had to do was skim the chapters right before a test to get As.

I didn't know it at the time, but my mother was concerned that I might quit school. She was a high school counselor, and had heard of a small liberal arts college with a higher academic standard. She suggested I apply to start there my sophomore year.

When I learned that as an English major, I could study for a semester in Oxford, England through a program at the college, I was thrilled! I'd never been to another continent, and I dreamed of traveling.

I got a school loan, and secured a work-study position at the school. Then my world turned upside down.

My parents told me I would never be able to support myself with a degree in English, and I needed to pursue a science degree instead.

I believed them.

My dream of taking English literature and writing classes at Oxford disappeared. Against all my inner intuition and knowing, I changed my major from English to Geology.

I hated it. I discovered that the cost of not being true to myself was clinical depression. Some days I couldn't get myself out of bed to go to class. My soul would have none of it. I couldn't make myself do it.

When the first semester was over, I told my parents that I wanted to switch back to English.

"You need to give it more of a chance. You can't know whether you like it after one semester."

I sublimated my own will for the second half of the school year. In the spring, I finally called home from a pay phone, in tears, and said "I don't care if I starve! I'm an English major!"

Good for me—but the damage was done. No Oxford. A wasted year. Depression. But worse, I let it mess up my thinking for a long while. I ignored my deeper intuition and feelings to follow some surface logic that I didn't even believe in.

I know my parents meant well. Their inner dragons were telling them I wouldn't survive if I got a degree in English. That was the prevailing belief at the time: English majors couldn't get a job, and liberal arts colleges were undervalued.

I did survive, and I ended up working good-paying jobs as a technical writer, and then as a people and project manager. But it put me on a trajectory of an inauthentic life, making decisions while ignoring my intuition.

Not following my calling to get my Ph.D. and teach and write creatively cost me a lot, on more levels than just my career.

There's a cost to answering your calling.
There's an even greater cost to not answering.
This is the point in the path where you need to choose.

Our Wounds Are Our Teachers

The universe uses our mistakes to help us get back on track. The decision to take the wrong path was like a grain of sand inside of me. It grated. It was painful.

But it also created the longing that brought me to seek out deeper growth, that kept me writing to stay connected with myself.

And more importantly, it showed me where I needed to grow. After all, I could have taken a stand and spoken up nearly a year before I did.

And my dear, sensitive, soulful creative, if you don't answer your calling today, then leave the door open to answer it later.

If you need support, get it.

Because your dreams aren't "nothing," or unrealistic. Your dreams are why you are here.

Growth is a process, not unattainable perfection. So be kind to yourself. When you make a mistake, it means you tried to do something before you knew how to do it. That's all.

I know that you know this, but it's always worth saying: You belong here.

We want—and need—your gifts.

Exercise: **Answer the Call**
1. What is the cost of answering the call?
2. What is the benefit of answering the call?
3. What is the cost of not answering the call?
4. What is the benefit of not answering the call?
5. Are you ready to answer the call?
6. If you are not ready, what do you need to become ready?

    Are you sure you're not waiting for the "perfect time"? (There is no perfect time.)
7. If you are ready, what is one thing you will do this week to get you moving?

Diving into the Mystery

*"You've been walking the ocean's edge, holding up
your robes to keep them dry.
You must dive naked under, and deeper under,
a thousand times deeper!"*
Rumi

My mom's health had been fragile and in decline for several years. While I was in the process of making big changes in my life, she passed away. Because she had begun to develop dementia several years earlier, I felt I'd actually begun to lose her well before she left this Earth.

My mom was brilliant, and a voracious reader. When I was in my forties, I remember her telling me about something she'd read in a memoir by a female writer. The author wrote that a woman's life doesn't really begin until her mother dies. I asked her if she felt that way about her mother—my beloved grandmother.

She thought about it, and then said, "Yes, to some degree."

I tried to imagine my life without my mom, but it did not feel like a beginning. And I wasn't sure why she shared that with me. Was she asking if I felt my life was constrained by her?

Yes, in some ways, it was.

Because she was my mother, my interactions with her gave me my first experiences with someone else's inner dragons. When she was feeling vulnerable, she could be temperamental and critical. As a child, I learned to take her emotional temperature before I entered a room, so I could avoid her sharp tongue.

But I also blossomed in the freedom she and my father created for me in the first five years of my life. Much of the foundation I built in thinking for myself was possible because I had the time and space to be, think, and feel, when I was so open and receptive to my connection with the universe. I truly felt in love with this world, and nothing interfered with that.

We are all so complex, filled with vulnerabilities and defenses.

My mother and I shared the trait of high sensitivity, which made us aware of things that others didn't always notice. Often, we knew what the other was going to say before we said it. I've never had that level of intuitive—almost psychic—connection with anyone else. And it meant so much to me.

Perhaps, not having my mother's critical voice challenging me, nor her intuitive insight supporting me, is part of making this path my own.

Maybe that is what the author meant all those years ago: when you lose your mother, even if you've been an adult a long time, you are initiated into the next phase of claiming your own inner authority.

Through the grief I've felt at not being a mother, and in losing my mom, this book has given me a way to express my deep desire to nurture and give to others.

Still, this is not what I wanted. I know that my mom would have loved to read this book, that she would have had insights for me—and I think she would have been proud of me. But this is my path, and I accept it for what it is.

Sometimes, our allies are in the spirit world.

CHAPTER 14

Creativity Is Transformational

Just as you use your imagination and materials to create something new, the process you follow to create transforms you. When you go to the deep place of creativity, subtle yet profound shifts occur.

You take action from your being—who you are. By taking action, you create change; you grow into who you want to be. The process of being, acting, and becoming is a circular pattern of growth that spirals upward from your center, whether you are painting a small watercolor or creating a new life for yourself.

There have been many times my path has brought me to a deep, dark place in my soul, where the twin dragons of regret and resentment taunted me that I'd wasted my life, that it was too late—and too difficult—to change.

That was nonsense, of course. But it didn't feel like nonsense when I was in the grip of those dragons. It felt very real, as though I was being pulled into watery depths against my will, unable to see very far or breathe deeply. At these times, I felt I was at the brink of a bottomless abyss; my feeling of hopelessness was nearly unbearable.

Thankfully, I've lived long enough that I know if I let myself cry, if I let myself feel angry or lost—if I feel whatever grief is demanding my attention—a shift happens. It gets better.

Diving into the Mystery

That's because being in the depths is part of the profound process of being alive. There is a spiritual purpose to dark nights of the soul. In the depths, there is treasure—and transformation. Much creativity and wisdom comes from this deep place.

When a deep, soulful tide pulls at my heart, demanding my attention, I don't know when the currents will sweep me out to sea; all I know is that trying to avoid the pain doesn't work. Because pain arises from meaning, and we cannot escape the deep meaning of this world.

When I accept that I have no control—rather than resisting the flow—the tide eventually brings me back to the clean, wide beach of my mind. There, I discover treasures brought back with me, like shells deposited on the sand. I am different, and perhaps a little wiser.

As the pain fades in my memory, I am left with something valuable. A deeper understanding of myself, others, and the world. This is when I am buoyed by meaning. This is when the words flow.

This is what makes it all worthwhile.

CHAPTER 15

Here Be Dragons

The phrase "Here be dragons" warns of dangers in exploring the unknown. In medieval times, mapmakers sometimes included drawings of dragons or sea monsters in uncharted areas. Or they drew the edge of the known world, the sea flowing over it like a waterfall.

In the Hero's Journey, the hero must slay a dragon to reach his destination. It's a useful analogy for the very real psychological process we go through over and over again, often with the same dragons, throughout our lives.

There are many times on your path when you must face your dragons.

What Is an Inner Dragon?

I use the term *inner dragon* to refer to the negative—often, bullying—inner voice that we must get past to create our art and live our lives authentically. Its mantra is: "You can't."

"You can't write a book; you don't have enough time."

"You can't start a business; you don't have enough money."

"You can't paint; you don't have enough talent."

Inner dragons focus on lack, keeping you stuck in the fear of never having enough, never being enough. In reality, you have abundant creativity at your disposal.

Inner dragons are sneaky. Often, they take a sliver of truth and exaggerate it into a fierce, fire-breathing roadblock. They can present the most convincing arguments by picking and choosing points of truth and mixing them with jumps of logic and exaggeration. You believe them because they reflect your deepest fears.

How Does an Inner Dragon Come into Being?

We come into this world with innate abilities, such as the ability to draw or a way with words. But when others in our lives fail to appreciate (or worse, mock) our gifts, we learn that it is not safe to share them. A sarcastic sibling, critical parent, or shaming teacher can plant seeds that develop into the voice of our inner dragon.

We learn all sorts of "lessons." That others aren't trustworthy and safe. That the world is a dangerous place. That we are not good enough.

The challenge in dealing with inner dragons is that sometimes their comments contain just enough truth to be convincing. Some people aren't trustworthy and safe. The world can be a very dangerous place. And we are all flawed.

What do you do when some of the most treasured parts of yourself are threatened? Much like the story of the golden Buddha, you hide those parts of yourself to keep them safe:

> Once upon a time, a village with a golden statue of Buddha was threatened by an advancing army. To protect the statue, villagers covered it in mud. Because the soldiers couldn't see its value, they left the statue alone.
>
> The war lasted for many years, until the villagers forgot about the golden Buddha beneath the dried mud. One day, a little boy was walking past the statue when a piece of mud cracked and fell off, revealing the gleam of gold underneath.

He ran to the center of the village, and told the others what had happened. They removed the rest of the mud, finally restoring the statue to its former glory.

This is a beautiful analogy of hiding our divinity—and our gifts—within ourselves to keep them safe, and reclaiming them years later. I don't think it is an accident that in the story, a child discovers the golden statue. We were children when we began to hide our light, and it is the child within each of us that longs to let it shine again.

There is a golden Buddha inside of you. This is the treasure that your dragons are protecting.

The Process

In my twenties, I took a trip to North Carolina, where I rented a small house on the beach with a couple of my friends.

One night, a boy knocked on the back door. He asked us to turn the porch light off, because there were baby loggerhead sea turtles hatching from a nest near the back of the house. The baby turtles rely on moonlight reflecting from the waves to find their way to the sea; any light coming from homes near the dunes confuses them.

We immediately turned off the light. Then he asked if we wanted to come down to the nest and see them hatch.

Of course we did!

About six people stood near the nest. Some kept crabs from nabbing the turtles as they made their way to the surf. Others stood in the water with flashlights, to guide the little turtles to the sea.

Small turtles kept crawling out of the nest, awkwardly making little "tire tracks" in the sand, as they struggled to get to the water. I was deeply touched by their vulnerability—they were only the size of a quarter!

I was also moved by witnessing part of their bigger journey, a pattern that has repeated over and over, for 40 million years. Those little creatures were propelled by instinct—by who they were meant to be—

to begin a journey that most of them would not survive.

The baby turtles who survive the gauntlet of predators swim to the Sargasso Sea, where they spend their adolescence in the relative safety of the seaweed. They "disappear" for safety and nourishment while they grow into adulthood.

When the turtles are big enough to survive most predators, they venture out into the open ocean. Eventually, they mate, and the females return to the beaches where they were born to lay their eggs.

Then, the process starts all over again.

Watching this ancient process gave me the sense that sea turtles remake the world, over and over again. I'm speaking metaphorically, of course, but literally, too. We are all making and remaking the world as we live our lives.

And there is a moment in our early lives, when we too swim to an inner Sargasso Sea, where we hide for safety. Parts of our psyche dive into the subconscious, waiting until we're ready to bring them back into the light, to "birth" a new insight, or to express our creativity.

The trip to our internal Sargasso Sea begins with our core wound.

Core Wounds

I believe that we each have a core wound that is the catalyst for our most profound growth and our deepest purpose. I am not saying that the wounding is good or right. Some people have been wounded from truly evil actions.

But being human in this complex world means that wounding is inevitable, even when you have "good enough" parents and a safe childhood. When we come into this world, we are so vulnerable, like baby sea turtles. Events that wouldn't threaten us as adults can feel like life-and-death situations to children.

The key to growth is how you transform that core wound into wisdom, so you can share your wisdom with others. The challenge is to move from the perspective of being a victim—or a failure—to being a creator, someone who faces her inner dragons, to make from her life something profound.

My core wound affected my voice; I learned not to say what I knew. Yet some of my greatest gifts are my intuition, my empathy, and my ability to communicate. My core wound forced the wisest parts of my voice underground. I've known my whole life that reclaiming my voice was something I'd have to do eventually. I had the sense that, over and over, I was failing a crucial life test. I've had to face my fears to reclaim my soulful voice; in fact, I'm still in what I believe to be a lifetime process.

There is a reason that our most inspiring stories are about people who overcame huge obstacles to achieve what their souls called them to do. If the purpose of our core wounds is to create deep transformation so that we can bring our profound wisdom into the world, experiencing the stories of others who were successful gives us hope that we can be, too.

Setting the Course

We don't want these wounds. We certainly don't deserve these wounds.

Yet as painful as they are, as much as they often mess up our lives or send us into therapy, they are universal experiences of being human. They are the dark side of our North Star. They are the hole we seek to fill, the meaning we fear is absent or unknowable.

How do we heal these wounds?

I don't have the answer; each of us, like our experiences, is unique.

But I believe that our core wounds set each of us on a course for consciousness and transformation. Eventually, they bring us to the brink of the abyss. When we're ready, we peer over the edge into the darkness. What we see there is the answer to the question we are most afraid to ask: is my life meaningful?

In my darkest nights of the soul, I would often walk right up to the edge, but refuse to peer in—not because I was afraid of what I would see, but because I was afraid of what I wouldn't see.

Do we fear the monster hiding in the closet, or the void—the threat of nothingness—behind the monster?

One evening while getting ready for bed, as I walked into my bathroom, I listened to my inner dragon's taunt that my life was meaningless; nothing had turned out the way I wanted it to. I remember the cold white linoleum beneath my bare feet, the pale bathroom walls surrounding me. I knew I had to relinquish my resistance to my greatest fear, or it would continue to control me. And so, some small, scared part of myself said, "Yes, I will look, no matter what."

And I did. I faced the potential utter meaninglessness of my life.

First, I saw emptiness. But then, something curious happened. I sensed something behind the void—below, above, everywhere. I intuited a meaningful structure holding all of existence. I reconnected with what I knew as a child, when I was so deeply plugged into that universal structure on a much deeper level.

To make sure you understand, I have not gone through life depressed and dour. I have always been able to experience awe at the deep meaning of this existence. But over time, I lost the ability to hold onto it. I could only see it in moments of grace, which seemed few and far between.

And it wasn't like everything was "fine" after that moment I looked into the abyss and rediscovered the unconditional meaning of my life; I've had plenty of dark nights since then. I've had to face this again and again; I've had to feel what I didn't want to feel.

Yet even though the difference was subtle, it was genuine. It was like I'd gained just enough spiritual resilience to take the next step, and the next after that. Because I knew what I'd experienced as a child was still true; it was real—even though I couldn't find the words to fully explain it.

It is the threat of the void that can show us just how meaningful our lives truly are, and that we each have something to contribute to this world. And to choose the good, to choose to serve, to choose to make a positive difference in another's life—however small—fulfills a blueprint of meaning in a context far more vast than our own lives.

As a creative person, living authentically is being of service to others, because you act as a beacon. Your inner strength and energy act like a magnet, helping others align with their true selves, too. I have experienced this directly through the goodness of my father and grandfather. Their alignment with the deep goodness in this world has helped me align my own inner compass, over and over. Who we are, and how we live our lives, matters.

Your Soul's Agenda

We all have core wounds, and the loss of faith or trust—in ourselves, in others, or in God and the universe—is at their center.

I believe that it all comes down to reclaiming our trust, our faith, in the deep meaning of this world. Even when we can't see it. Not that everything will work out the way we want it, although it may. But that who we are, our character, matters.

I believe this, because I had to lose my trust in myself, in others, in life, in God—and then find it again. I had to experience living conditionally, to more deeply understand what as a child I knew was true: life is made of unconditional meaning.

When I stopped demanding that life, or people, or God, "show me" that they were trustworthy, ironically, I became more trustworthy. I stopped hedging against imagined negative outcomes, and "keeping my options open" for a way out. I learned to trust myself to be able to respond creatively to whatever life brought. Trusting myself has given me the freedom to accept life and others, whatever comes, in ways that I could not before.

I had to learn this lesson the hard way, over many years, in relationships and life situations. I now see that some of the most traumatic, difficult experiences in my life were, as Rumi said, the physician in me trying to heal myself.

Our souls make choices for us that are intended to help us wake up—even the "wrong" choices. Our souls don't care how difficult it is; that's not their business. Their purpose is to be real. When on the surface our choices seem "wrong," there is often a deeper agenda at work: becoming more conscious through learning the hard way. Life is creative, and in every situation, we have the ingredients to grow, if we choose to.

You are living your soul's story, regardless of whether you're fully conscious of it. And, your life is exactly as it needs to be, right now. You have everything you need to create what you want in your life.

The Gift of Waking Up

Some of your talents go underground—or swim away to your inner Sargasso Sea to hide, until you feel strong enough to bring them back to the surface. The gift of this universal process is that they are fresh, new, and ready to be actualized. It's time to develop them.

Being human is a profound process of becoming. It is a long path to recover our wisdom. We take what we did naturally as children, and learn to do it consciously. It's a deeper level of being and doing.

Most importantly, our wounds, when faced with an open heart, experienced, and processed, teach us compassion for others.

What Is the Purpose of an Inner Dragon?

I have a lot of shame about letting myself be knocked off of my creative path when I was in my twenties. I've had to face my inner dragon, over and over, to get through the process of writing this book.

If our core wounds are meant to wake us up to our deep potential and soul work by first putting us to sleep, then what role do our inner dragons play?

Ironically, they try to keep us asleep to save us from pain. They are the voices that whisper, "You are the mud, not the gold," because they believe if you share your inner gold, it will be taken from you. But it cannot be taken from you: you *are* the gold.

Although you can lose touch with the core of yourself and with your various shining talents, they are always there, ready to be reclaimed.

Your inner dragons guard your treasure-rich abyss. They stand at the portal of loss, at the threshold of grief. They try to keep you from crossing the threshold, to protect you from the danger your psyche perceives on the other side. Because unprocessed grief holds you back, you have to feel your grief for the lost parts of yourself, and then let it go, to be able to reclaim them.

That inner dragons taunt you to keep you from your treasure seems counterintuitive. But here's what I've discovered: repeating negative thoughts actually feels safer than facing the original cause of the pain.

The question is: which pain do you want to feel? The pain of regret over things you didn't do, or the pain that allows you to reclaim those parts of yourself so you can express your gifts?

Magic Spells

The repetitive, negative tapes of your inner dragon act like magic spells that hypnotize you, keeping you asleep, unconscious. They obscure the shining truth of your gifts. To reclaim the parts of yourself you've hidden to keep them safe, you must undo the "magic" you used to create them in the first place.

Although your outer dragons may have many faces—the negative judgment of your family or friends, or a toxic coworker—in the end, the dragon you face is your own self-doubt: your fears about your own talent or worthiness.

I realize I've just offered your inner dragon a tasty morsel of guilt. Don't swallow it. You are the heroine—or hero—of your own life. If you haven't accepted that yet, chances are you're waiting for something outside of you to save you—a knight in shining armor, or a winning lottery ticket, perhaps.

Mine was a vague hope that somehow things would work out. Maybe something outside of me would change, and I'd spend the rest of my life happily writing, traveling, and painting—without a care in the world.

Maybe, indeed.

Here are just some of the magic spells your dragon may use to stop you:

"It's too late."
"I'm not talented or smart enough."
"I'm too sensitive."
"My voice isn't important."
"Success is for other people."
"I'm too weird; no one will understand me."
"I don't have enough time."
"If I go after my dreams, I will let others down."
"I don't have enough money."

Exercise: **Recognize Your Inner Dragon's Magic Spells**

It helps to get clear about which dragon spells are gripping you in their sharp talons. That gives you a little objective distance to reality-check the magic spell. "Is this true?"

1. What are some of the things your inner dragon says that keep you from doing your creative work?
2. How does your inner dragon show up in other areas of your life?
3. Does your inner dragon use the same or similar ploys to keep you from taking risks in your creative expression and in your life?

    What are those ploys?
4. What antidotes can you use to move you past your dragon?

The Truth About Inner Dragons

When you accept that dealing with your dragons is actually part of the process, and that you are your own heroine—or hero—on your creative path, you realize that your "failures" are what you need to push against to build strength and resilience.

Expecting yourself to face no roadblocks or hardships in your quest to live your authentic life is a false perspective. It's simply not realistic. So, arm yourself with fierce self-compassion, and the willingness to keep going when you can barely see what's possible, as you put one foot in front of the other.

As you consciously venture into the realm of your inner dragons, it's helpful to be clear about what your inner dragon is, and is not.

Your Shadow Side and Your Dragon

The psychologist Carl Jung said that the qualities we judge to be inferior or wrong become part of our "shadow"—behavior that we disown. Our shadows are our "dark sides," which we are often not conscious of. Our dark sides may appear when we use drugs and alcohol, or when we are stressed and tired. Or when we're driving! When I'm cut off in traffic by a driver with a "Coexist" bumper sticker, I have to smile to myself.

Our dragons guard what Jung called our "white shadows," the parts of ourselves that are not negative, but that we have disowned as if they were: gifts such as our voices, our creativity, our wisdom.

Projection is when we unconsciously—and usually vehemently—project our own negative shadows onto others like old movie projectors. Sometimes, the other person exhibits the dark qualities that we repress. That makes it easier to scapegoat them, and remain unconscious of our own darkness. I know I may be in the grips of my own shadow material when my emotions seem exaggerated for the situation, especially when accompanied by black-and-white thinking.

We also project our white shadows onto others. For creatives, we do that with artists. The artists whom you strongly admire tell you something about who you are and what you value. They may also be clues as to your unlived gifts.

These treasures are the parts of yourself that you need to bring back into the light, into the conscious creativity of your life.

Just like integrating (but not acting out) our dark-shadow material brings us consciousness and depth, reclaiming our white-shadow gifts supports self-actualization. And it brings those gifts depth and definition.

The Difference Between a Dragon and a Perspective

A dragon is a negative inner voice that taunts and berates you into giving up. It tests your faith in yourself, and helps you to build confidence by facing your deepest fears, over and over. When you say horrible things to yourself, you're in the talons of one of your inner dragons.

A perspective is a way of looking at the world. It is influenced by your beliefs and experiences, and either supports or hinders you. It is broader than the focus of an inner dragon, and is mostly focused on the outer world.

When you find yourself generalizing about people, places, or life, you're expressing a perspective.

"Starving artist" is a perspective. "The world is creative and abundant" is a perspective. Our perspectives can support or challenge our dragons. That is why it's so important to be aware of your perspectives, and to choose those that are most supportive.

Is It Your Inner Editor, or Your Inner Dragon?

How do you tell the difference between your inner editor and your inner dragon?

The tone of your inner editor is neutral: "This part is effective; this part still needs work." It's just information, and you may feel mostly encouraged, because you now know what to do next.

The tone of your inner dragon is bullying: "This is the dumbest essay in the world. No one wants to know what you think. You have nothing to say. You can't paint. Your music sounds like nails in a cement mixer. You have no talent; you're kidding yourself. Give up!"

See the difference? Your inner editor focuses on what you need to tweak in your poem, your photograph, or your clay bowl before you fire it.

Your inner dragon focuses on the *value of your work*—and ultimately, the *value of you*. And it exaggerates shamelessly.

Sometimes, the inner dragon inserts itself into the voice of the inner editor, derailing your ability to be objective. That's when you need to walk away, and come back to your work with fresh eyes.

Look, we've all seen people who have a higher opinion of their abilities than is realistic. For example, the tone-deaf singers hoping to make it big on talent competition shows.

And I've written stories I thought were pretty good, until I received feedback from people who were more experienced in the craft.

We all need feedback and editors to help us hone our craft. When you're ready, get feedback from others whom you respect. Just don't let your dragon convince you to conflate your skill level and abilities with your self-worth.

How to Deal With Your Inner Dragon

A core wound is the lack of faith in the creative potential of life: "I'm not enough; others aren't enough; the world isn't enough." *The answer to this wound is to create anyway.*

That requires facing your dragons.

Remember: using these strategies won't destroy your dragon. They may get you past it. Over time, you will build the consciousness and resilience to face your dragon in whatever ploy it uses on you.

Practice Self-Compassion

There is no way you can live life—let alone blaze your own Creative Heroine's Path—without practicing compassion for yourself when you're hurting. You must forgive yourself for making mistakes—in other words, for not knowing something before you knew it, or not following your intuition when you didn't have the strength to do so. It's the pain of failure that teaches us at a whole other level what something means to us.

You aren't here to live someone else's life. You must first accept yourself as you are to become who you want to be. I realize this is easier said than done, and like everything else, it's a process. But if your inner dragon's words pummel you until you are a puddle on the floor, you must deal with it.

If you wouldn't say to a friend what you are saying to yourself, then stop. When you catch yourself doing it again, *stop!* Look at yourself through loving eyes. You have to practice self-compassion. No one can hand self-acceptance to you. You must take responsibility for what you tell yourself.

Self-compassion and self-forgiveness are critical. Without them, you're in hell, and transformation is not possible. Compassion and forgiveness are not just ideas, but are real transformative states. Grace is the ultimate response to our inner dragons: the chance, however briefly, to see ourselves as God might see us.

Sometimes, when I'm doing something ordinary, like standing in line at the grocery, I'll really look at the faces of people around me. When I do that, I see their beauty. I feel compassion and love for them. In those moments of grace, I feel that I am being given the gift of seeing through God's eyes.

When a friend says something awful about herself—her appearance, her talent, her worthiness—you may feel her comment as an arrow that pierces your own heart. You probably jump to her defense, because you see the beauty of her spirit shining in her face. It's there; you see it!

And when you say awful things about yourself, your friend sees your beauty. If what you see in her is true, then what she sees in you is true also. Remember that. Others can act as mirrors for ourselves, if we choose to accept their words.

Defy Your Dragon

Taking action is the antidote to your dragon's "magic spells."

If your inner dragon keeps telling you that you cannot write, draw, sing—however you express yourself creatively—remember Van Gogh's words: "If you hear a voice within you say, 'you cannot paint,' then by all means paint, and that voice will be silenced."

If you hear, "I don't have enough time," commit to an amount of time you do your creative work each week—and stick to it like your life depends upon it. Whether it's an hour a day or an hour a week, you will move forward.

And if your dragon tells you, "You don't have enough money," invest in yourself anyway—enough that it is a stretch but not a hardship, so that you take your dreams seriously.

Dance With Your Dragon

Dancing is a give and take; you don't banish your dragon, you simply practice holding your own with him. If you think of it as a kind of dance, that might help you understand that it's not about controlling your dragon. You hold a space of calm in the center of yourself, while the fear and confusion swirl around you.

When I'm in the grips of one of my dragons—such as financial survival—my shoulders and back tense as though I'm in a defensive position, preparing to be attacked. And of course, I am. In fact, I'm already attacking myself mentally—telling myself I'm not safe, that I'll lose everything.

That's what dragons do. They jab a sharp talon into the sensitive center of one of our most basic existential fears: that there isn't enough.

This is when I consciously deepen my breathing, down into my belly and solar plexus. This helps me relax my shoulders and back. Then, I slowly turn and face what terrifies me. I begin a "dance" in which I practice holding my own space so that I can still move.

My fear, my dragon, doesn't leave me. But we move in a mutual agreement that we both can exist at the same time. This helps me practice being with my fear without letting it paralyze me.

Unmask Your Dragon

There's a scene in the movie *Van Helsing* where Frankenstein's monster is attacking Anna Valerious. He's been hunted by villagers who want to kill him, and he sees her as an enemy. When he has her cornered and it looks like he is about to kill her, she suddenly asks, "What do you want?"

This completely disarms the monster. "I want to live!" he cries, showing his human side.

Something trapped behind your fear wants to live.

There's often a grain of truth in what your dragon says. It's usually a matter of degree and leaps in logic that create the lie. What is the kernel of truth in your dragon's taunts? When you address that, the dragon will quiet down, because it has your attention.

Ask your dragon what it wants you to know. After all, it is guarding treasure from your past. This part of yourself knows the profound value of what it is protecting.

When you understand what your dragon is trying to "save" you from, the tension shifts, and you can move forward. You can address the kernel of truth to reach the treasure.

Like Frankenstein's monster, the parts of yourself that doubt, that tell you that you have nothing to say, or have no talent, or aren't worthy enough to express your voice in this world, have something to tell you. Perhaps their message is that sharing who you are will change your life.

When you face them, you are looking into a mirror that projects your fears. Take a peek behind the mirror. What are you afraid of? The voices of doubt have something to tell you. The human face behind the mirror isn't as scary. She will let you pass.

Stand Up to Your Dragon

Stand up to the fear, in whatever form it shows up for you.

One trick I use to give me the courage to face a fear directly is to imagine how I would feel if someone I know and love was beating herself up the way I am. I would be incensed and indignant. I would stand up to the dragon, if it were bullying someone I loved—or anyone, really. We have to learn to be our own spiritual warriors. This little thought exercise helps me remember to be my own advocate, not my nemesis.

It's the way Gandalf sets a boundary to save his friends in *The Lord of the Rings* by saying, "You shall not pass!" to the fiery Balrog.

It's easier to stand up to your dragon if it's in the service of something bigger than yourself. Tap into your courage to help someone else, then use it to help yourself.

Treat yourself as well as you treat others.

Deflate Your Dragon

Don't give the dragon your attention and energy. Snub it. Redirect your attention and focus on something else. It will deflate like a balloon, because it's really only hot air anyway.

My Boykin Spaniel is not a dragon. She is, however, a bit spoiled. When she wants something from me, she'll begin to cry. Softly at first; then she starts to warble. She makes the most pathetic sounds. And she gets to me every time! (She knows it, too.)

When I steel myself and refuse to respond, after a little while, she gives up. But if I look at her and respond in any way, she ups the drama.

There's truth to how energy feeds off other energy. When I don't give her any more of my attention, she can't keep it up; her energy deflates.

So, if it helps, think of your harping dragon as my spoiled dog and remember not to give it an inch, or it will take a mile!

Puff Up Your Dragon

This probably feels counterintuitive, but if you're feeling strong enough, try agreeing with your dragon—to the extreme. When you reach the level of absurdity that makes you roll your eyes or laugh at yourself, you've made it.

Because when you're trying not to feel your fear, your emotion gets stuck. If you blow your fear up like a balloon, it will burst.

One of my most persistent dragons has been the fear of taking financial risks to reach my dream. It's not funny; I can be brought to tears and immobility by this fear. When I'm firmly in its grip, I agree with it, taking the negative possibility to the extreme.

When I exaggerate my fear to its endpoint, I think "If I try to live my authentic life, I will end up a bag lady on the street." That's when I begin to roll my eyes. (Most of the time!)

Letting myself feel what I'm afraid to feel—to the point of absurdity—helps release the more intense emotion, and then I can see it in a more balanced way.

Prove Your Dragon Wrong

In general, it's difficult to argue with a dragon, because dragons aren't rational. But, sometimes logic can help a little. When I catch my dragon in an exaggerated absurdity, sometimes I can fend off its illogic. If you can't do this alone, gather your allies.

When I was struggling to reorganize and clarify some concepts in this book, I was getting nowhere, and I felt lost and discouraged.

Here's a sample of the "conversation" I had with my inner dragon (though it feels more like a monologue, because we hear our inner dragons' voices as our own):

"I'm a talentless hack who has nothing worthwhile to say."

(That kind of exaggeration was a clue that I was in the grips of my inner dragon.)

"I can't do this. I'll never finish this book. And then everyone will know what a fraud I am."

"My mind isn't good enough. I have too many thoughts that lead to nowhere."

"I'm going to let everyone else down. I'm going to let myself down."

"I should just give up. I want to give up."

I decided to reach out for help.

I told my husband that I was struggling, and he reminded me not to "abuse" my creativity. (Don't you love it when others quote your own advice to you—advice that you are clearly not following?) He reminded me that I am a good writer and have valuable wisdom to share. He told me to stop pushing it and let it go until the next day. It was good advice, to give myself permission to take a break.

I also contacted a dear friend, a painter who reminded me that she attended my retreat and my 10-week workshop—and she left both of them feeling inspired, with new connections, visions, and artistic endeavors. She asked what I was struggling with, and she offered to meet for coffee and lend me support.

Sometimes, you need your "champions" to remind you that you really are talented and worthy, and that you have something valuable to say.

Don't wallow in the muck with your inner dragon. If you need support in proving it wrong, reach out to your allies.

The Question Life Asks of You

Your core wound is, ultimately, a question that Life asks you. It makes you question yourself, and it brings confusion. You can't see it clearly, although you experience its effects acutely. It's like a spot that always stays in your peripheral vision. You try to get it into focus, but it keeps moving just to the edge of your sight.

My core wound was a silencing of parts of my voice—my inner knowing. When I was little, I didn't identify with Cinderella or Snow White; I identified with the little boy who says the emperor is naked, in Hans Christian Andersen's *The Emperor's New Clothes*.

But I learned not to say what I knew.

Writing this book and speaking about it are keys to reclaiming my voice. They are some of the ways I am answering the question Life asks of me: "Will you stand up to your dragon? Will you show up? Will you be seen?"

Yes, I will.

It's up to you to answer the question, whatever it is. This is your calling—your call to grow and to serve. You learn the answer by going into the dark forest, venturing into the depths, showing up and being seen, developing your voice.

Push against your own inertia, take imperfect action, and do it anyway, even when you believe you can't. Even when the mute child within you feels like you will die if you do it, despite what your rational mind is telling you. Because that's how bad it feels. That's how scary it is. Those are the stakes. Like any heroine, you must face the dragon to claim your gifts, your wisdom, your life.

And then, you give back. Because to be on this Earth, to see the sky, watch the trees waving in the breeze, smell the salty ocean, see the vista from a mountaintop, hold the tiny hand of your child, love your soul mate with all your heart—is a gift. Rumi was right; when we're depressed, we're throwing our lives away.

Don't waste another day living someone else's idea of your life. Start taking imperfect action, one step at a time. You will get there. Have faith. The world needs your gifts.

CHAPTER 16

Into the Abyss

The abyss is a place of deep feeling and profound transformation. It is a murky inner sea, filled with intense pressure, hot volcanic fissures, strong currents—and deep, creative magic.

When you're in the abyss, you feel stuck and hopeless. You're lost in the dark, despairing, afraid, and utterly alone. It is a place beyond logic, beyond words, and beyond your control.

Yet this is the place of growth and wisdom. It is the depths of your subconscious, the mysterious place that holds all your experiences. And it is where you touch the collective unconscious, the archetypal stories of humanity. When you are pulled to the abyss, something is preparing to come into your consciousness: an insight, a new idea, an intuition, a way forward.

In the abyss, your carefully constructed framework of reality doesn't make sense. The signposts on your map disappear, and you stumble off the path. You wander around in the dark, overwhelmed and feeling lost. You fear you will never find your way home. You don't want to be there.

Yet it is exactly where you need to be. This is where magic lives.

This is where you swim in the most profound meaning of your life as you face the unknown, process your grief, and transform your life experiences into insights—or art.

Something Needs Your Attention

When you enter the abyss, it's because something within you needs to be made conscious. This is deep soul work, where you are either pulled into the depths by a spiritual process, or by choosing to dive.

You choose to dive when you go to a counselor to deal with trauma. Or when you take an honest look at your relationship with someone, to cleanly and clearly initiate a conversation with him or her about a difficult subject.

You also choose to dive when you pick up a paintbrush and shut out the world, or when you pick up your pen and begin writing whatever comes to you.

When you consciously choose to dive, the filter of your mind is like a diving mask that lets you see clearly, but with some distance. You do this whenever you think deeply about a life situation or a creative project. It's fascinating, because you can tap into not just your own wisdom, but the collective wisdom available to us all. And your mental "mask" serves to shield you to some degree from the more difficult emotional flotsam.

But as a creative, and a human being, you don't always get to choose when you dive. In those instances, it can feel more like a hand rising from the depths, grabbing you by the ankle, and pulling you under. This experience doesn't feel like the focused inner exploration when you choose to dive; it feels dark and murky. Your energy drops; you feel helpless and lost. Your will is weighed down by a stubborn inertia.

I call it "being in the soup," because I know I'm being "cooked"—transformed by the heat and pressure. Then, when it's ready, an insight will emerge, changing my perspective. Changing me, just a little bit at a time.

When I'm in a dark, hopeless place, I often resist it, trying not to feel the despair that overwhelms me. Over the years, I've learned that when I'm able, it's best to just be in the soup. For me, it seems to shorten my time in the abyss.

If you never let yourself be with your own grief, fear, or anxiety, you block the transformation needed to access the deep wisdom that is available to you. The purpose of this particular pain is to wake you up to deeper meaning.

And facing what you don't want to acknowledge gives you something to push against. It helps you build the necessary spiritual muscle to be with what is waking you up. I see it as a necessary part of the path to living deliberately, consciously, and authentically.

When I accept, and choose to dive and go with the flow, transformation happens. This is the process of growth, of creation and wisdom.

Here's the key to being in the abyss: let go of your desire to control everything you're experiencing, and be with whatever comes up. Because this phase is about transformation, and the creativity that flows from it.

Feeling Lost

When you're making art, your mind and your subconscious play together.

When you write, the narrative of your story—or the structure of your ideas—emerges with just enough surprises to keep you curious.

It's like walking in the dark, while your mind strikes matches and tosses them in the direction that leads you to the heart of what you have to say.

But sometimes, you just feel "off." You can't seem to muster much enthusiasm. And you can't seem to write, paint, or create anything worthwhile. Sometimes, when I try to write anyway, I push through the inertia, tap into a current, and the words flow.

But other times, nothing works. When that happens, I need to sit with my mood to give it a chance to tell me what I need to know. Moods are messengers, and when I'm feeling seriously blocked, something needs my attention.

I resist the temptation to pretend I'm not feeling lost. I don't dust my mood with sugar sprinkles. Don't get me wrong—I value positive thinking—but not as a diversion to keep me swimming "safely" on the surface.

When life gives you platitudes, dive into the profound.

(Yeah, I just wrote a platitude.)

It's uncomfortable. I fidget a lot. If I'm not careful, I'll unconsciously try to drown my discomfort with a chai or a cookie. Or TV, Facebook, the latest *New Yorker*. Or outrun it with activity, like vacuuming or going to the store.

But when I shut down the computer, put away my phone, turn off the TV, put down the magazine, stay put in the chair, and simply notice, I'll find a lot there that I haven't wanted to feel. Grief. Fear. Confusion. Anger. Doubt.

Mixed in is the overwhelming desire to know everything will be okay, that I won't fail. And behind it all is the existential whisper, "What if it's all for nothing?"

I know that everything won't always "be okay." And I know sometimes I will fail. And existential angst will grip me many more times in my life.

These are the times to be with my vulnerability. Instead of trying to rise back to the surface, I need to feel the pressure, my shallow breaths, the tightness in my back against an unseen future swimming up behind me.

Where I'm feeling most vulnerable is a passageway to honesty. I know at some point, I'll notice something bright and intriguing, and follow it to the surface. If a subtle current brushes against my skin, I'll listen; if a thought, an intuition, a feeling brings me buoyancy, I'll listen.

But until then, I sit in the deep. This is where the real words come from, if you stay curious and open. Before you can describe the light, you have to brave the darkness. This is the difficult and exciting part of being alive, and finding your true voice.

Listen to what you have to say, especially when it's just a whisper.

When you push up from the bottom, you might find that your fear and uncertainty bring poignancy and meaning to your words, floating beside you, up to the sun-dappled surface.

Transforming Your Experiences

I have a love/hate relationship with "positive thinking" and "affirmations." When they feel genuine, that's wonderful. But when they don't, trying to force myself to feel something that I don't feel is—to borrow a term from the great Julia Cameron—"crazy-making."

You probably know someone who puts on a false positive front, and you can feel the cognitive dissonance a mile away. I know whenever I try to force a positive mood, it feels so icky that I have to stop.

When I was little, and I was especially worried about something bad that might happen, I would go to my room and let myself imagine the worst. That may sound masochistic, but that wasn't the intent—or the effect.

I am deeply feeling, highly sensitive, and empathic—sometimes, a bit psychic. I don't remember the incident that prompted it, but one day when I was around seven years old, I was standing beneath the maple tree in our back yard, upset because I believed my family thought I was "too sensitive."

As a child, if I merely thought that one of my parents might be angry with me, I was devastated. (So perhaps they had a point.) I felt that when I became a grownup, I was expected to be less sensitive—hardened, even. Under that maple tree, I made a vow to myself to never let that happen.

I knew that I had to be strong to be sensitive. In fact, I knew that I was already strong. Because I didn't want my fears to control me, I would let myself feel whatever came up—in a private setting—to build up my emotional muscle. It helped a lot. Whether or not my fears came to fruition, I kept building my resilience and strength to continue to feel as deeply as I felt.

In those moments, I also learned the alchemy of fully expressing emotion. I learned why it's bad to short-circuit the process.

I knew I wanted my life to be as real as possible. I wanted to be completely here in this world—even during the difficult experiences.

Besides, when I'm not letting myself feel something, it's like it's always in my peripheral vision, following me. You can't escape yourself, so you might as well be present.

I believe that the purpose of emotion is to viscerally process and transform our experiences. When we're being real, our bodies are like musical instruments, vibrating to the experiences in our lives.

That's why creativity is so essential to living a full life. Taking those moods and emotions, transforming and grounding them in something tactile, is healing.

If you feel bad, feel bad. If you feel angry, feel angry. If you feel grief, grieve. If you need support to safely process your more painful emotions, get it. Because your mood is trying to tell you something about the deep meaning of your life. If you don't feel it, you won't learn what it is.

You may know someone who thinks her bad mood entitles her to make everyone around her feel horrible. That is not what I mean. That's acting out the mood instead of processing it. It's abusive, not only to other people, but to the message her mood is trying to give her.

Try channeling your mood into your creative expression. Paint a bad painting. Write a bitter poem. Sing off-key. Let your art transform your mood into a place of deeper understanding—something real.

The Meaning in Suffering

When I was in high school, I discovered Viktor Frankl's *Man's Search for Meaning*. It was extremely helpful to me. When I saw so many kids in school using alcohol and drugs to avoid experiencing their pain and confusion, I knew it was not only futile—you cannot escape yourself—I also believed it was damaging. I felt that trying to manufacture bliss was the toxic mimicry of true spiritual experience.

It seemed to me—and still does—that we already have everything we need to experience awe and meaning in this world; we have only to be fully present to know it.

But I had reached a point where I started to question my faith in goodness in the world.

I had read Anne Frank's diary, and could not ignore the horrifying dissonance between her words—*In spite of everything I still believe that people are really good at heart*—and what happened to her.

As I learned about Nazi atrocities, the Trail of Tears, and other acts of cruelty and annihilation, I could not pretend that evil did not exist. Yet it was in stark contrast to my experiences of God, and of the unconditional meaning and love in the world.

Even without evil, the suffering we experience can leave us questioning not just the meaning of our lives, but of life itself. Frankl's experiences in a concentration camp taught him that finding the meaning in his life gave him strength—even to endure the worst suffering. He believed that the one thing that cannot be taken from any of us is our ability to choose our responses in life. This is key.

The meaning in suffering is personal; no one can tell you what your own suffering means. But being fully present and alive in this amazing world requires each of us to take a stand for or against meaning—not necessarily in God or a religion (although those are often part of the context), but whether or not there is meaning to our lives.

I believe the world is made of meaning. The matter and energy in this physical existence also serve as metaphorical blueprints for spiritual truths. One simple example is how relationships need to develop deep roots to withstand life's storms, like a well-rooted tree.

There is so much creative wisdom in this world available to us.

Whether or not you believe in life's existential meaning, it's up to you to find the specific meaning in your own life. And as difficult as it is, you experience that meaning not only in joy, but in your suffering, in the loss or threatened loss of what matters deeply to you.

I try to look at my own suffering within a bigger context, because that is the only way it makes sense to me. I trust that something wants to be made conscious or stronger within me. Even when it makes no sense, or isn't fair, or is the result of evil actions, I trust that there is some meaningful context for me. Why? Because that is the only perspective that helps me grow and keeps me from falling into despair.

And I also believe it.

Carl Jung said that basis of all mental illness is the avoidance of legitimate suffering. With the exception of physiologically-based mental illness, I agree with him. I'm not saying that suffering is good, or that we deserve to suffer. I'm saying that it is inevitable, and it requires a conscious response from us.

There's a great line in the movie *Home for the Holidays*, where Tommy says about his sister, Claudia: "She'll bounce back. Trust me on this. No, she feels her feelings. But she'll bounce back. Feelings come up and she actually feels them, which is great."

When I can, I try to choose to respond to my own suffering by being with it long enough for internal alchemy to happen, and wisdom to surface. When I can't, I ask God for help in doing that. Often, what feels like help from the invisible world shows up in a quiet, internal voice reminding me of something I'd forgotten about the context of my life.

But I don't always do that. Sometimes, I try to avoid uncomfortable or painful feelings through watching TV, or eating when I'm not hungry. There is a myriad of ways we avoid feeling our feelings when they actually come up—through alcohol, drugs, food, shopping, social media, TV, computer use. We may even try to run from it through excessive busyness, or involving ourselves in unnecessary drama.

When I avoid dealing with something, it's always about trying to stay "in control." Whether life circumstances or someone else's action have "taken" your power, your ultimate power is in how you choose to respond.

This is the key to responding creatively to suffering: be fully present to your joy and sorrow to find the hidden meaning or wisdom waiting for you.

How to Be in the Abyss

Just like a physical wound, where our bodies redirect energy and resources to help it heal, our psychic energy is pulled to our emotional wounds. It's what happens when you get pulled into the abyss.

When I'm in the abyss, I feel lost and hopeless. The pain can be so acute that I can't be fully present in my day-to-day life, because deep processing is happening.

The abyss is not meant to be a dwelling place; the pressure is too intense. It is meant to transform—not drown—you. When I stay too long in the abyss, I am depressed. At those times, I see my life through the lens of being a victim—or its self-flagellating cousin—a failure.

Seeing the bigger context and self-compassion are a team of perspectives that can support you during your time in the abyss.

The bigger context reminds you that you're there again (ugh!)—but it won't last forever, even when it feels that way. And it is a necessary part of being human; it is deeply meaningful. A part of your consciousness is going through a real transformation, and if you stay in it, if you pay attention, you may bring back an insight or inspiration for your next short story.

Self-compassion is key, because you are most vulnerable to your inner dragons when you're in the abyss. This is the time to stop telling yourself that you are not good enough, or strong enough, or smart enough.

You are needed in this world.
What you bring into this world matters.

Emotions Are Weather

Your emotions are meant to move through you, leaving clarity and freshness in their wake, like a spring storm.

When you let yourself really feel what's going on underneath—instead of just acting out your initial reaction—you can experience a kind of alchemy, where something unconscious shapeshifts into wisdom.

However, when your emotions don't move through you, if they get stuck, you experience a mood. Moods are messengers. They are emotions stuck in a pattern or loop. Something either needs your attention or is in the process of transformation.

We are like little one-person sailboats, bobbing on an uncertain sea. We're on the surface, profoundly affected by the weather and the currents. We float on a vast depth that we guess at, or intuit, or experiment with.

When your little sailboat is on rough seas, being buffeted by strong winds, pay attention. What is the message for you? Sometimes, you can avoid having that hand reach up from the depths and pull you under.

Dealing with Anxiety

If anxiety interferes with your ability to live your life, seek professional support. The material in this section is not a substitute for professional help designed to support you in your particular circumstances.

In the abyss, anxiety and depression are like twin tigers circling, ready to pounce. Although depression dwells in the deepest part of the abyss, anxiety lives there, too. It's like your psyche's last-ditch effort to not feel what you need to feel, distracting you from the real issues with peripheral fears.

From my experience, knowing and working with other soulful and creative people, I've learned we're wired in sensitive ways that allow us to bring treasures and insights from the depths, which we use in our art and in our lives. However, sensitivity can feed anxiety.

Anxiety is diffuse fear. Its tendrils reach out from your chest to the top of your head and the tips of your fingers and toes. Then, it constricts, as if those tendrils are being wound tight from the center of your chest.

Your back and shoulders tense. You can't get a deep breath without consciously working at it. Your stomach cramps. Your head aches. Forget sleeping. Forget concentrating. You are frozen in a defensive position.

Or those tendrils vibrate like electric wires, broadcasting obsessive, negative thoughts, as you fidget and try to run away from the experience.

When you're in the grip of anxiety, you're in deep emotional suffering. Your spirit is struggling. You can hardly get anything done, because the inner processing is so intense.

You could sum up the perspective of anxiety as "I'm not safe." And when generalizations like that become a foundation for other perspectives, it becomes crippling.

When I'm in the grip of extreme anxiety, I feel like I'm not going to survive it. It shuts my creativity down. When I'm anxious, I try to remember to flow like water, or to ground my energy.

Flow Like Water

When anxiety manifests in your body as a rigid defense against the unknown, your muscles tighten and your breathing becomes shallow. You feel unable to move, to take action. As long as you are frozen in a defensive position, it's difficult to deal creatively with the situation.

When you accept your life as it is, you work with the creative flow. And the more you flow with life rather than against it, the more you access your wisdom—and are able to create from that.

When you're feeling tense and anxious, it's a good time to ask yourself what you are afraid to lose. Your fear is like a big boulder in the middle of a river. When you cling to your fear of losing something you value, it can keep you from seeing potential resolutions just a little further along the path.

Take some deep breaths. The universe is abundant and creative. You have resources at your disposal to respond creatively to whatever is making you anxious, but you won't see them until you flow around your fear.

When necessary, make a conscious choice to forgive others and to forgive yourself—for mistakes, selfishness, the unconscious behavior that brings so much complication to our lives. Holding onto resentment is the same as holding onto fear. It holds you back.

Ground Your Energy

When anxiety manifests in your body as a nervous, crackling energy, you're moving as a defense, like a boxer dancing in the ring. When your body won't settle, when it's tense, fidgety, and painful, try grounding your energy.

I love the phrase, "ground your energy." It's a great analogy—just like you need to ground electric current, you need to ground your crackling mental thoughts when they're flailing around like live wires. It's like your mind is temporarily disconnected from your body and soul. Good luck finding any wisdom without them.

Grounding and getting present is key. When you're grounded, you can often hear your own inner wisdom more clearly. Try focusing on something tangible or meditating.

If you're still feeling unsettled and your mind is filled with negative thoughts, don't fight it. Just accepting that this is where you are at the moment can bring you calm. Trust that your soul is in a deep place; some process is happening deep within you.

Be gentle with yourself. Your personal best right now is the best you can do at the moment. Resilience ebbs and flows depending on the circumstances.

Exercise: **Ground Your Energy**
1. Unplug from all electronic distractions.
2. Take a few deep breaths.
3. Tap into your senses and notice the details of what's around you—see the sky, touch a leaf, smell the fresh air. Or sit and watch a fire in the fireplace, or a candle flame. Just be with it.
4. Get curious.

What does your strong inner core want you to know?

Dealing with Depression

If depression interferes with your ability to live your life, seek professional support. The material in this section is not a substitute for professional help designed to support you in your particular circumstances.

I've experienced depression multiple times in my life, either when a specific traumatic circumstance required most of my psychic energy, or when a series of losses built on one another before I fully recovered from the previous one.

During those times, I always felt like I would be stuck in that place forever. There was a time when I considered myself a "functional depressive," someone able to keep it together and fulfill my responsibilities, but with an underlying despair circling just beneath the surface of my life.

When the overwhelming feeling of hopelessness derailed me, and a heavy, numbing inertia kept me from fully living my life, I sometimes worked with counselors. Other times, I somehow climbed out of the pit on my own.

Over time, I learned that I could work with feeling stuck and with my own resistance, often with the love and support of others.

Being Stuck Is Just a Pause in Your Journey

Being stuck is difficult. I often think I "should" be able to keep moving through sheer will. But that is not only exhausting; it distracts me from what I could learn in a situation that is uncomfortable for me.

I love the film *The African Queen*. It's a classic hero and heroine's journey, set in Africa during World War I. Through a series of events, Charlie and Rose find themselves on Charlie's boat, the African Queen, on a mission to sink a German gunboat on Lake Albert.

If you look at the story metaphorically, Rose represents our higher selves—our inner wisdom—that not only knows what to do, but acts as a catalyst calling us to make the journey we must make.

As in any hero's journey, Charlie initially refuses the call. He's like the part of ourselves that thinks of a dozen reasons why something "can't work." Yet each step of the way, Rose is there guiding him, helping him see possibilities, and most importantly, teaching him how to believe in himself again. At times, he is angry with her, resenting how she pushes him to take risks and test his limits, when he just wants to stay safe and comfortable. But Charlie keeps pushing through his own doubts, moving toward the goal.

Pushing through your own resistance builds resilience.

After struggling and failing to free the boat from a muddy marsh in the Bora River (which flows into Lake Albert), Charlie tells Rose he must be honest with her: they're stuck. At this point, Charlie and Rose believe they have failed in their mission. But a bird's-eye view reveals that the lake is just beyond the marsh. They are so close to their destination, but they can't see it.

Accepting where you are does not mean accepting you have to stay there forever. It simply helps free up your mental and emotional energy to rise up over the "mud" and view the possibilities available to you.

And it's true. When you stop struggling and digging yourself in deeper, you are no longer focusing on what's not working, but opening up a door for what will work.

While Charlie and Rose sleep on the boat, rain falls into the Bora River until the water lifts the boat out of the mud, over the marsh, and into the lake. They're free from the muddy marsh, able to continue on their mission.

Don't forget providence. Don't forget allies. And don't forget how strong you really are.

When you're feeling stuck, remember it's just a pause in your journey. Be curious about what a "bird's eye view" can reveal about your situation.

Trust that challenges are there to help you grow, whether beyond a limiting belief, or simply to learn new skills.

All the doubts, the fear, the negative voices are a normal part of pushing beyond your routine and into the unknown. Resistance and challenges are what you push against to grow your spiritual muscle, to build resilience.

Working with Resistance

The ebb is a natural pause in the dance. You feel constrained and you can't get anywhere. Your subconscious—which co-creates with the muse—is holding back to process and regenerate, and to get clear on the mark. If your mind takes over and tries to force it to happen, you will miss the mark, again and again.

Your resistance means something. But what?

Why, when writing feels like plugging into the electricity of the universe, when composing a song makes you crackle with purpose, do you sometimes resist doing it?

When you're stuck in the kind of resistance that keeps you from doing something you really want to do, it feels like you're fighting an invisible force inside yourself.

So, what is that force, exactly?

Think of an archer pulling back on the string of a bow, increasing the energy to propel the arrow toward the mark.

The arrow is anything you intend to do, like writing a new story. The mark is the target you're aiming for, like completing a first draft.

Resistance is the part of taking focused action where you pull back a little and pause. It helps you gather energy and get your target in sight.

So, resistance is actually helpful.

However, when you hesitate past the moment when your energy and focus are in alignment—past the moment when you need to take action—you lose energy and focus, and you may give up.

Remember that it's simply one moment in a process. When you feel it, think of it as a messenger telling you that you are poised to act. And you are the archer. You are the one in control of how far back you pull that string, how long you take aim, and when you let that arrow fly.

When resistance shows up, don't overthink it. Give yourself some time, and when you're ready, make the conscious decision to let go.

When You Can't Do It

There were times when I was writing this book, which I very much believed in, that I couldn't work on it. It felt flat. The well dried up and the meaning was gone.

When this happens to you, let go. Don't try to force it. When something wants to be brought into the world through you, you can't make it happen before it's ready.

Stop, take a walk, sleep on it overnight, and start fresh the next day. You meet your creativity halfway by showing up, so when the mysterious workings of the muse and your mind and intuition meet to begin the dance, you're ready.

When I find myself rebelling, it usually means I've neglected something that wants and needs expression. So, when I'm blocked, I write by hand about how I'm feeling. There's something about putting pen to paper that restarts the flow for me. (Especially if I'm using a favorite fountain pen with purple ink!)

Just as a field needs to lie fallow for the soil to be restored, creativity needs that time, too. Here are three ways to support yourself while you're enriching your creativity.

Let Go of Expectations

When you're in a gestation period, you need to let go of your expectations of yourself. Life and creativity aren't about being productive 24/7. They both require rest and play.

If you ignore that need, and demand of yourself that you constantly produce—and that it's always "perfect"—you're abusing your creativity. You'll burn out, just like soil leeched of nutrients.

Forcing yourself to be productive is fruitless. Let it go.

Listen to Your Whispering Voice

You know what to do; you just have to give yourself the time and space to hear yourself clearly.

Turn off the TV, put away your phone, and unplug the computer. Get outside and take a walk by yourself. Notice things. Stop and look up at the leaves on the trees. Pay attention to the ground beneath your feet. Take in the scents around you. Listen to the sounds of being alive.

Journal with no end in mind: just see what flows from your fingertips and follow your inner wisdom. Or sketch whatever is in front of you.

Seek Out What Inspires You

Go to a play, a concert, a reading, an exhibition. Read literature. Go to a great, old book store and browse. Sit in a chair and sample a book or two. Read a poem.

Resist the tyranny of a clean house. Regardless of whether the furniture is dusty or the floor needs to be swept, time is passing. Nourish your spirit first.

Let other kindred spirits who have tapped into their own wells help you tap into yours. Replenish your creative soil—and your soul.

And always remember: be kind to yourself!

CHAPTER 17

Discovering Your Vision

I had a vision of this book before I had the details. I knew I wanted to write a book about creative expression and living a creative, responsive life. I didn't know what this book would look like, but I found myself thinking about how messy my own creative process felt, and I wanted to put it in a context that made sense to me. Over time, *The Creative Heroine's Path* emerged.

What is your vision? It could be as specific as a single poem, or as broad as a new business to support your creativity. It could be an idea you want to express, or an emotion or experience you want to convey. It could be your soul's purpose. It's something meaningful to you.

It could be your love of color, or shape. It could be functional art, such as pottery. Or music that resonates in the center of yourself, and that vibrates in others in response.

Developing your vision is an iterative process. You bring up treasures like pieces of a puzzle, one at a time. You may not know for a while what the final form will be. But the clearer you are on the overall purpose, the more motivated you become.

Catching Insights Like Fireflies

While I was writing this section, my eye caught a glimpse of leaves on a bush outside my window, illuminated by sunlight. They were gorgeous and bright green, surrounded by dark green leaves fanning out where the branch was in shadow.

Then, a cloud passed over the sun, and they lost their definition; all the leaves became a dark green mass.

This is what it's like with insights; they glow so brightly that you think you will still be able to see them clearly if you look away for a moment. But the moment passes, and they're no longer clear.

Often, when you have an insight—a shift in perspective, a deeper understanding—or you see in a flash what you need to do with a scene in a story, or you realize what needs to change in the composition of your picture—it can fade quickly. Like a dream, it's a shadow that mists in and out of your waking mind.

That's because your insights are from a deep place, accessed through your subconscious, and your conscious mind doesn't have a frame of reference for them—yet.

Whether you're aware of them or not, you operate from beliefs that shape your view of reality. New insights that challenge your current view of existence won't "fit" until you expand your worldview.

Just like you create routines that allow you to more or less automatically navigate your life, your conscious mind constructs a framework to make sense of your experiences. This is your worldview, your global perspective, from which you assign meaning to the events in life.

When an insight comes to me in the regular course of my life, I often need to experience it a few times, over a few months or years, before I can keep the insight in my consciousness. Each time, I am able to hold it a little longer, until my perspective finally grows to support it.

I've had insights where I saw things so clearly that it was a profound shift in my world view. I've written them down, only to come back to them later and not understand what I meant.

That's one of the ways I learned about perspective, and how when you can't hold onto an insight, or when it doesn't make sense the next day, it means you just don't have the mental framework to support it—yet.

Until your perspective expands to hold your insights in your consciousness, you will fall back to sleep again and again. That's okay. Until your worldview expands to support your insights, hang onto them. Write them down, or capture them somehow, because they are the architecture of your deep wisdom.

Exercise: **Keep Insights in Your Awareness**

Things will always conspire to keep you asleep.

When you have an insight—something that you need to remember to stay awake to your inner wisdom—try grounding it in art.

1. Paint your insights—or do calligraphy, or write them on a yellow sticky note in messy ballpoint pen. Just capture them.
2. Put them where you will see them last thing before you go to sleep, and first thing when you wake.

The Pearl

People put a lot of effort into trying to feel happy, satisfied, and content. Or to not feel anxious, depressed, or empty.

But dissatisfaction is like a grain of sand irritating the soft body of an oyster: it provokes a response. In the case of the oyster, the irritation produces a pearl.

I believe our responses to the basic existential challenges of life are meant to create something valuable, too. Our dissatisfactions are challenges to grow, stretch, and push out of our comfort zones.

So, what's behind the dissatisfaction? For me, it was the call to step away from the status quo and toward the authenticity of my inner wisdom.

On the surface, a frustrating situation may seem like a condition imposed on you from the outside. But if you listen more closely, you can often hear a deeper calling for change, or expression, that you need to honor to grow.

There have been times in my life when, instead of seeing my dissatisfaction as an invitation to make a change, I've focused on the grain of sand, not the pearl. And the grain of sand is what we can't change. It's there to provoke us to grow. Focusing on the grain of sand can make you feel helpless, and even more frustrated. But when you focus on the pearl, you're responding, you're creating—you're both responsible and free.

Sometimes, I didn't want to be responsible and free. I wanted to be comfortable. I wanted something outside of myself to change so I wouldn't have to.

You can guess how well that worked.

You've probably known someone who complained about her circumstances but did nothing to change them. I've been that person at times in my life. At those times, I was so entrenched in my negative perspective that I couldn't see my way out.

Dissatisfaction calls to us to look deeper. But it can be scary to dive so deep that you brush against your own monsters, that you lose your sense of what's up and what's down. So, we "stay busy." We tune out. We complain. Or we focus on everything that was wrong, is wrong, or could go wrong.

Often, friends and family give us lots of sympathy in response to our complaints. It just seems easier to blame the world than to grow ourselves.

For a while, it may be easier. But in the long run, it's harder, because we keep ourselves stuck and guarantee that we keep having the same type of experience over and over again.

Choosing to respond creatively to something we are dissatisfied with makes all the difference.

Exercise: **Find the Pearl**

1. In a challenging situation, can you think of a time when you focused on the "pearl"—the outcome you wanted to create—rather than the "grain of sand"?
2. How did thinking of the pearl change that experience for you?

    What did you learn?
3. Now think of a "grain of sand" you are currently experiencing in your life.

    What creative response is it trying to evoke in you?

    What is the potential pearl in the situation?

Follow Your Lodestar

This is a good time to check back in with your lodestar. It reminds you what matters, and inspires you to take your insights from the abyss, and get clearer about your vision.

Exercise: **Check In with Your Vision**

1. Look at the insights you've captured after you've been in the abyss lately.

    What do they have in common with each other?
2. Look at the values in your lodestar.

    Do you notice a theme between the values in your lodestar and the insights you've been having?

    What else is coming up?

    This is a good time to journal about it, or create a vision board.

Creating a Vision Board

To create the life you want to have, you need to envision that life. The purpose of a vision board is for you to get clear about your vision, and keep it in your consciousness.

Think of it as a mirror image of your goal, a reflection of your dream.

I don't think making a vision board is "magic," where all you need to do is create one, and *poof!* your life magically changes. In fact, that view almost held me back from facilitating vision board workshops.

That said, I realize that some people swear by them, having synchronistic experiences of getting what they wanted soon after making one. I am not one of those people.

I believe when you create a vision board and changes happen in your life to support that vision, several things are influencing the positive outcome:

You believe your goal is possible. Concretely visualizing your goal helps you to see and feel the potential, while bypassing some of the negative inner voices that nip your dreams in the bud.

You clearly see what you want. Choosing images brings clarity, which goes a long way to helping you make the best choices to support your vision of a creative life.

You tap into your excitement. As you find images that resonate with your vision, there's real energy around making it happen. Enthusiasm opens the door.

You take a step toward owning the commitment. Making your vision real requires commitment. And when you are committed, providence moves to support you.

You accept that you are not in control of what happens. You play with images that you find in a magazine, creative elements that others have brought into the world. When you accept that you are co-creating with the universe, it removes the pressure caused by the belief that you have to do everything yourself. You have some influence, to be sure, but when you let go of what you don't control, you free up mental energy.

You go with the flow. By circumventing linear thinking as you play with images, you discover intuitive, holistic insights. Logic is an extremely important tool, but overusing it or using it too soon can keep you from seeing the creative ways that something can happen. When you follow your own intuition, you can better take advantage of opportunities as they arise.

You do the work. When you put your vision board where you see it every day, it not only reminds you of what matters, the images you chose begin to seep more deeply into your unconscious, influencing your choices and your beliefs about what is possible.

But, I have my woo-woo side too. It makes sense to me that making your vision into a tactile, visual representation is an important, symbolic middle step between your idea and its manifestation. You have to be able to visualize something before you can make it real.

Exercise: **Create a Vision Board**
1. Gather and look through magazines, search online, or even use old photographs.
2. Notice what you resonate with.
   Select and cut out images and words.
3. Play with possibilities.
   Arrange the images and words on the poster board.
4. Create your vision.
   Paste the images and words on the poster board.
5. Discover the themes, connections, and patterns.
   See what "jumps out" at you.
6. Focus on your insights.
   Put your vision board where you will see it every day.
7. Act on your wisdom.
   Make choices and take steps that support what you truly want.

Sharing Your Gifts

*"The meaning of life is to find your gift.
The purpose of life is to give it away."
Pablo Picasso*

The migraines started a week before I was to appear onstage. It was going to be my first public appearance to talk about my creative vision—this book—and I was petrified.

I'd given presentations and training in front of large groups before, but this was different. This time, I would be talking about a very personal experience. It was a level of vulnerability I usually reserve for close friends and family.

Shortly before I was scheduled to speak, I sat in the auditorium listening to another talk. Suddenly, I felt ill. I knew it was a migraine. My composure crumbled as the migraine brought me disorientation and pain. A sense of helplessness washed over me. I felt utterly vulnerable and alone.

I realized that I was facing a very old fear of being seen, and criticized. And I knew that I had to face that fear. I understood that the experience—as horrible as it felt—was a necessary gift.

Later, moments before I was to walk onstage, I literally felt as though I was going to die. But, I went onstage anyway. I spoke about how changing my life saved my life. I spoke about this path, and about writing this book.

I was certain that I sounded ridiculous.

Guess what happened? Afterward, several people came up to me to tell me how much what I had said touched them. I didn't fully believe them at first. Then, logic drowned out my inner dragon. It was a valuable lesson.

By sharing my gifts, I had taken the first step toward developing my voice as a speaker, and I had connected with people.

This is what it's about. Growing and connecting. Making a difference.

CHAPTER 18

Creativity Is Inspirational

Your gifts matter. They give insight, inspiration, comfort, beauty—even utility—to others.

What would it feel like to write a song that you played only in your head? It would be like a symphony playing in a locked, soundproof room, with no one to hear.

If no one experiences your creative expression, no one can be touched by it.

When I write, it is a solitary endeavor. But at some point, I need to share what I've written. Not just for feedback, but to connect and to share who I am.

We take from the moments of our lives the raw material to form something new. When we paint, a bit of our soul is transferred into the brush strokes, in the wash of colors.

When you develop and share your gifts, you are giving in a powerful way. You touch people beyond your circle of family and friends. This is profound.

Creative people who are also caretakers often think they're being "selfish" when they take care of their own needs—let alone follow their calling.

If you're struggling with this, let me offer you a new perspective: When you follow your calling—when you write your novel, paint your masterpiece, sing your soul—and share it with the world, we all benefit.

That is what I mean when I say, "The world wants—and needs—your gifts!"

My life, your life, everyone's life is a journey of discovery. We're all exploring some facet of the universe, using the gifts we bring to this world. When we share them, we enable others to look through the lens that we see through, and perhaps, to be with and transform their own pain.

When you share your gifts, you develop your voice and connect with kindred spirits.

Experiencing Creativity

Creativity is the mysterious process of taking an experience, an idea, or an inspiration and transforming it into something new.

Whenever you create, a little bit of your spirit is infused in what you make.

The first time I saw Van Gogh's paintings in person, I became quite dizzy.

On a trip to Paris in 2003, I visited the Musee d'Orsay. When I entered a room full of Van Gogh paintings, it was my idea of Heaven on Earth! I slowly walked through the room, looking at the paintings. Then I stopped before one, riveted.

Near the top of the canvas, Van Gogh had used paint strokes so thick they curled like tiny yellow tongues. When I looked at them, I felt dizzy.

I averted my eyes for a moment. Then I looked at the painting again, my knees wobbly, my vision blurry.

I bent my head down and steadied myself.

When I looked up at the painting again, I felt that I was seeing the passion in life itself. I sensed a brilliant blue energy, pulsing like a star in space.

When I turned and slowly walked on, I found my eyes drawn back to that painting several times, as if by looking one more time, I could understand the brilliant blue heart that had painted it.

(I have a confession: although I described the thick yellow paint like tiny yellow tongues in my journal, I did not capture the name of the painting! I was so overwhelmed in the moment, that it didn't occur to me until later. I believe that painting was *Pine Trees with Figure in the Garden of Saint-Paul Hospital*.)

Art is not only something we see or hear or make, it is also an experience that activates something mysterious inside us. Art is more than just "communication." We create something that gives others a glimpse of our souls. This is the spirit infusing creative expression. The boundaries between us become translucent. We *see*.

Some of these experiences are deeply profound. And when we are deeply moved, we are transformed.

This is the value of your voice.

Art as Catharsis

Creativity is a doorway to your soul. It is filled with the essence of something deep inside you that wants to be seen. Your imagination and skill work with your experience, distilling it into its essential form. In this way, you create your unique expression of a universal experience that others can relate to.

When others move through this doorway, they are changed. When your creative expression resonates with universal human experience, it brings us back to our own unique experience, which we see in a new way.

This process is so organic and part of who we are, that it feels magical at times. It takes disparate experiences, consciousness, skills, and materials, and creates something related, but new. It changes—for the artist and the observer—how we feel and how we see. Making and experiencing art illuminates the meaning beneath joy and suffering.

CHAPTER 19

Finding Your Voice

Finding your voice encompasses both speaking from what you know deep inside, and experimenting with your creative expression. It's about learning to discern the false notes from the true.

As you take your first steps, you may find and lose your way over and over, but as you recommit to your path, your unique and creative genius begins to emerge.

No one sees the world exactly like you do. No one else looks through your eyes, no one else shares your mind, your soul, or the experiences that make you who you are.

Don't worry about making something original; what you make will be as unique as you are.

Don't ever talk yourself out of doing something because someone else has already done it. *Of course* someone else has already done it! That's not the point.

The point is: *No one else can do what you do, the way that you do it.*

It's Your Path

If you compromise, if you express your calling in a way that you think you should, rather than what comes authentically, you lose the power that comes from following your passion and purpose.

We've all done it: tried to do something in a way that we think will impress others, or to meet their expectations. When we do that, it always comes out flat and uninspired.

For years, I thought I couldn't paint, because I thought paintings had to be realistic. I tried to draw and paint in a way that was not natural to me, but more importantly, in a way that didn't interest me at all. My paintings contained no energy, thus perpetuating my belief that I was not talented enough.

But still, I had the desire to paint, and when I let myself play, I discovered that I liked to paint stylistic flowers and shapes, and use lots of color.

I called them my "little paintings," ostensibly because of their size, but really, I was belittling them first, before anyone else could—to let others know that I knew they were inferior to "real" art.

Imagine my surprise when the few people I showed them to really liked them. Enough people said so, and in a genuine way, that eventually I believed they weren't just "being nice."

I began to look at my paintings differently. I accepted their beauty and form. I was proud of them.

I wasn't trying to be or paint like anyone else.

Then, I got my first commission: to paint sunflowers. That would never have happened, had I not shared my "little paintings."

So keep going, keep practicing, and trust that the world wants your gifts!

Claiming Your Inner Authority

Your voice is like a fingerprint. Its tone and its cadence vibrate to the rhythm of you. You are the author of your life. As you express your true self, you begin to see the path forward. And your voice develops further, refining itself.

In our hardships, we find metaphorical clues as to how we need to develop. And I believe, ultimately, that what each of us is searching for, and is meant to express, is our own inner sovereignty—our inner authority to follow our unique paths. We're looking for outer permission when what we really need is inner permission.

"Finding your voice" means speaking up, saying something when it may be difficult. To do that—especially when you risk rejection—requires that you align with your own inner authority to form and communicate your ideas.

It also means developing your natural, authentic style, to communicate your vision and express your creativity.

Finding your voice involves aligning the "lens" of you, with your inner author, so that those who resonate with your gifts will feel them at a level beyond intellect. And that emotional experience has alchemical, transformational power.

Just like a song can take you to a place beyond words, you know it when you experience it. When others align with the lens of you, they are able to see what only you can show them.

You Are the Heroine of Your Life

What do heroines do? They create deep meaning from the ordinary clay of their lives.

Heroines exhibit authority. You are the authority—the author—of much of the circumstances in your life. When you take responsibility for what you create in this world, you are able to respond creatively to your outer circumstances.

Listen to your inner wisdom. As you hear your inner voice more clearly, your natural authority arises.

The Freedom in Responsibility

It's scary to take full responsibility for your life. It took an illness and a layoff for me to finally face up to the fact that there are no guarantees anyway; I might as well actively pursue my dreams, rather than trade them for "security."

I worried. What if I make mistakes? But, of course, I will and I have. We all do.

What if I experience losses? I'd already experienced losses; some outside of my control, others not. I'd rather reduce the regret in my life by taking responsibility for the things I can.

I needed a strong enough ego to live with that, which I am developing through facing the difficulties and building *spiritual resilience.* No one else can do that for me. If I asked someone else to work out so I could get stronger, obviously that wouldn't work.

Here is what I know: when you stop blaming other people and outer circumstances for staying stuck, you experience freedom. Freedom and responsibility are two sides of the same coin; they are inextricably linked. When you are responsible, you have the freedom to act, to fail, to try again, and to succeed.

Believing someone else owes you your life is a kind of tyranny. And it's an excuse not to try. Ultimately, it's a denial that you have created your life so far—and you are creating it right now.

If you are waiting for something or someone outside of yourself to magically change your circumstances, you will never create the life you want.

If you want to see magic at work, *show up.* Be open to collaboration. Find mentors.

It might seem impossible, but it isn't. You already have the seeds of potential inside you. As you grow into the person you need to become to live your authentic life and express your true vision, you awaken your potential. You do that by taking imperfect action, again and again.

Being Seen

A couple years ago, I attended a business workshop on authentic expression. It was challenging for me, because it involved talking about my creativity coaching in front of the group—on video—and watching the recordings afterward.

My most vicious inner dragon comments are about my physical appearance. And I had to face that. Although I was in my early 50s, I felt everything the average teenager feels: stupid, ugly—you name it. Not. Good. Enough.

I learned a lot about facing my fears and being vulnerable. When I'm playing and being creative, it's much easier for me to be myself. When I speak from my heart, the words flow. But when I'm worrying about what others are thinking of me, I'm awkward and miserable.

It is scary to embody who we are, because we risk rejection. Like me, you've probably buried parts of yourself, because you didn't feel safe enough to express them. But your strength is in your authenticity. When you're being who you are, doing what you are called to do, you can inspire others. You can make a difference.

It takes energy to hide parts of yourself. Holding yourself back from what you are called to do—from painting, or working in hospice, or coaching a softball team, any type of gift you have—is exhausting.

Silence takes away your voice, but also cuts you off from your wisdom. Self-censoring and hiding can make your connection with those parts of yourself atrophy.

When you create something you are proud of, or have an insight, there is a natural desire to share it. Because it has changed your life in some way, you want to offer that to others.

We're all instruments vibrating to our own inner truth. Others pick up on that. Quit hiding; people often feel the resonance of your truth regardless.

How do you know your gifts are valued? Because those who appreciate you act as a mirror, reflecting the worth of your gifts back to you.

The Power of Vulnerability

One of the things I've struggled with as a writer and an entrepreneur is showing up authentically. I'm good at the supportive, uplifting stuff. But sharing about the harder things activates all sorts of fears for me, and they all boil down to this: worrying about the judgment of others.

It just about kills me to admit that.

All my life, I've been proud of thinking for myself, not going along with the crowd. Peer pressure always seemed absurd to me. I think that when people try to pressure others to conform, it is often a projection of their own doubts about themselves and their choices. When you can see beyond the surface behavior to what's really going on, peer pressure doesn't have any power over you.

Which brings me back to caring about what people think.

Of course, I care about how people react to what I share. In fact, I want them to react, because I want to touch people in ways that make a positive difference, no matter how small, in their lives.

But the truth is, some people just won't relate to what I have to say. Others won't like it, some will misunderstand it, and everyone will have some sort of judgment about it.

The challenge is to show up anyway.

So, what is the power of being vulnerable? Of being authentic?

You may help someone. You never know who may be struggling with the same thing. Sometimes, just knowing we're not alone makes a world of difference.

Your authenticity shines more brightly. Some of the energy caught up in hiding who you are gets released into simply being yourself.

You gain resilience. When you practice good boundaries, and listen to your intuition about what you choose to share, and with whom, you learn that it's safe to be real. As others accept you for who you are, you learn to accept your own frailties, which strengthens you.

And the truth is, there are people who want to know who you are, what you think, how you feel. I'm thrilled to see the movement of energy in Vincent Van Gogh's paintings. I'm in awe when I read Rumi's poetry. I laugh out loud at cat videos posted on Facebook.

The perspectives we share with each other are like kaleidoscopes of meaning, little stained glass windows into someone else's soul.

They enrich our experiences on this Earth. They add depth, lightness, and beauty. And I am grateful for all of it.

How can you bring more of who you are into your self-expression? Now, what are you waiting for?

Don't Sublimate Your Soul

While I was writing this book, I had a profound experience. I revisited a time in my life when I had lost my way. For years, I had been telling myself that I could not survive financially by following my calling to write.

By the end of my corporate management job, my stress level was dangerously high, I was in near-constant physical pain in my hip, back, and neck. I was experiencing complete exhaustion from misdiagnosed pneumonia.

For the past couple of years, I've been reclaiming my creative life. This has required some uncomfortable shifts in perspective—and some leaps of faith. The closer I got to the deadline for handing this book off to the editor, the more I found myself in that old mindset.

I was approaching my calling the same way I used to approach my job, looking at life through a fearful sense of lack, and creating my own stress.

I went right back to where I was emotionally, near the end of my corporate job. I experienced the same physical symptoms. And I felt helpless.

I felt like I was going back through the same door into the past, through the same tunnel of negative perspective. I had to re-experience how that perspective left me stuck for years to discover a new way of living my life.

I was writing this book in much the same way as I had been told to handle projects in my job:

- Set a deadline unrelated to the actual time and effort needed to complete the work.
- Do a "good enough" job.
- Get it out on time.

I was sublimating the soulfulness, the meaning, the calling of my work.

Oddly, that's the very moment when I realized that this book had become a real calling, not just a means to an end.

I started writing this book because I wanted to develop online courses to support other soulful creatives on their path, and—gasp!—to make money.

There is nothing wrong with making money from your calling. But I was putting a strategy to support myself through my creative work ahead of the work itself. And everything inside me rebelled.

Now I realize that this is even more deeply true than I used to comprehend: everything in the outer world is a mirror of your inner world. If your soul is starving, you'll see the outer world as a dangerous place where you have to stay safe not to starve.

You can't force creativity. It's on soul time, not linear time.

And ultimately, it is your authentic voice that moves others.

CHAPTER 20

Connecting with Kindred Spirits

Sharing your gifts leads you to your kindred spirits, where you belong.

That group understands the value of what you do—and who you are. We all need to understand the impact of our creative expression in the world. It's not a luxury, or "nice-to-have" thing; it's essential. Feeling the appreciation of others for what you do brings fresh energy, meaning, and hope to your life.

There have been many times in my life when I needed a jump-start, a connection with kindred spirits to support me in my creative expression, and in living life more creatively.

Being part of a community of other creative heroines has been so helpful. Your group reminds you that you're on a path, and to have faith that you are creating the life you want—one day at a time.

How Art Connects

Art lets you vibrate in sympathy with what is experienced but cannot be explained. It's more than communicating "information." It's evoking an experience, which is a form of alchemy, in both making and experiencing it.

It opens a window between yourself and others, letting them see into you, into what you share with them.

Art is like a match struck in the darkness, illuminating part of the mysterious whole that is existence. It is so vast we cannot experience it all at once and have it make any sense.

Art illuminates one aspect of the mystery, and it is so satisfying because that one glimpse is itself whole and knowable. It is this deep meaning that we crave and need.

When you create from your heart, it feels like music. There's a vibration to your words that communicates through shared sympathy. It's more than just "processing," to use a psychological term. It's taking from your experiences, and from the deep soil of who you are, and creating something new.

Sharing Your Vision

When you share your vision, you change lives. You have an impact. You make a difference. And you give others the chance to appreciate your gifts.

That's pretty wonderful!

The appreciation others have for your gifts is a mirror they hold up for you, showing you the value of what you bring to the world.

And we need this from one another.

When we bring our experiences and insights back to the community, we are like creative shamans, bringing healing to others through art.

If you have something to say—and you do—we need to hear it.

We are your community. Experiencing your journey gives us hope. It helps us see we are all on our own journeys, and we are not alone.

The world wants your gifts.

Showing Up

Sharing my vision with other people, beyond the circle of my closest friends and family, has been both exhilarating and intimidating.

Exhilarating, because I love being an ally to other creative souls who need support on their paths. Intimidating, because—gulp—what if they don't like or don't care about what I have to share?

One of the most powerful pieces of wisdom I got from my coach is this: "People are going to judge you. They are going to have opinions about you. You have no control over it. Get used to it."

Yuck. I hate that. But okay, I get it.

Whether you share a poem, a painting, or a perspective, it will resonate with some people, and not with others. Your job is *not* to anticipate the judgment of others and adjust accordingly. Your job is to show up and be real.

Because that's what people need. And more importantly, it's what *you* need.

Paint a tree the way you see it. Write a story the way you want to write it. Share the ideas and perspectives that are uniquely yours.

You are not here to be anyone else.

What Happens When You Show Up

When you share your ideas and beliefs, your creative expression, good things happen!

You face your fears. You and your work will be judged. People will always have opinions about your work. You can choose to live under the tyranny of caring too much about what other people think of you, but if you let your fears run your life, you are holding your creative genius hostage.

You make mistakes. Each mistake moves you forward, showing you what doesn't work, so you can do what does work. A mistake means that you cared enough to try. Don't let it stop you. Your calling is too important to undermine it with perfectionism!

You get it right. Success reminds you: *you have this.* You *can* do this. You *are* doing this. And remember, when something goes wonderfully well, take the time to celebrate it. This is extremely important! Honor your successes. Don't brush them off.

You learn about yourself and others. You learn from your own insights, and from others pointing out your brilliance and your contradictions. For creative heroines who want to grow and self-actualize, this is a wonderful by-product of taking a stand—artistically or otherwise.

You open the door to prosperity. You can't make money from your creativity if you don't share it with others. Let's be honest: being prosperous means living a life that is full of what you love. And when you make money doing what you love, that's the best! You may be surprised at how many people want, and see the value of, what you have to offer. Give them a chance to show it!

Exercise: **Share Your Voice**

1. Share something of yourself with someone this week.
   A poem, a thought, a sketch.

   If you're up for a "triple-dog dare," share this with someone new, whom you haven't yet allowed to see this part of you.

2. What did you share?
3. What was it like for you?
4. What was it like for the other person?
5. Look at your lodestar.

   Take a few moments to appreciate its beauty. This is some of what others get from you, just by you being in the world. That is a beautiful gift!

Coming Home to Yourself

*"If you do follow your bliss you put yourself on
a kind of track that has been there all the while,
waiting for you, and the life that you ought to be
living is the one you are living."*
Joseph Campbell

The process of writing this book has been enlightening, hellish, fun, frustrating, inspiring, drudgery—in other words, a lot like life.

There were many times I told myself that I couldn't do it. When it was difficult, I didn't want to do it.

I struggled. I missed deadlines. I received glowing, encouraging feedback. It was not an even, simple process.

But I kept coming back to my original intention for changing my life: I had a vision, and I wanted to make it real.

The most challenging perspective for me was to be able to trust that it would all work out. To trust in my own ability to do it, and that I had the resources to finish it. And—to trust that what I share will matter to someone.

Writing this book brought me home to myself, through reconnecting with my inner voice, facing my fears, and focusing on the positive.

Reconnecting with my inner voice was like sorting through a box in the attic, tossing out what wasn't me and keeping what was.

I gained resilience by facing my fears, over and over again.

I relearned to focus on the abundance and creativity in life, rather than the limitations. And I found that what I focused on slowly grew bigger in my life.

If you were to ask me who I am at my core, I immediately think of myself when I was a little girl, standing beneath the branches of my favorite maple tree. I see light and shadow rippling on the ground from sunlight shining through the green leaves. I see myself, looking up into blue sky visible through the branches—fiercely in love with this world.

To be alive, to feel tapped into the universe, to take from my life and create something meaningful, has brought me home to myself.

And to be sharing my soul's intention with you is a gift beyond words.

CHAPTER 21

The Courage of a Heroine—or Hero

It takes the courage of a heroine (or hero) to create a work of art—or an authentic life. Despite the opinions of others, you trust that you have something valuable to share. You take imperfect action, when you cannot see the other side of the proverbial forest. In the thick of things, often without a clear direction, you create anyway.

To go deep and make of your experiences something new, and to share it through your art and the way you live your life, is to risk ridicule or indifference. But you do it anyway, because to live your life inauthentically is not an option.

Everything you create, each poem, each painting you share, is a beacon for others who resonate with you. It helps us find each other, our direction, and our deeper purpose for being here.

Before I had named the Creative Heroine's Path, I attended a gathering at an Emerging Women's Power Night. At that event, a local artist was selling jewelry designed for female entrepreneurs. She had a silver pendant engraved with this Joan of Arc quote:

> "I am not afraid; I was born to do this."

Those words pierced my heart; my eyes filled with tears. I was surprised by the intensity of my reaction; the quotation resonated deeply within me.

"I am not afraid" echoed how I feel when I am actively connected to the meaning of what I do: courageous and committed. It also reminded me how I feel when I'm not connected: afraid, lost in the forest, and alone.

But it was the declaration "I was born to do this" that prompted my tears. As I write this, I am still deeply moved by those words. What I was born to do touches the core of why I write and paint, why I wrote this book, and why I work with those who want to live their creative lives, in whatever form is meaningful and resonant to them. I have the sense of being in service to something bigger than myself.

At the center of the pendant is the outlined shape of a woman pulling back on a bow and arrow. She's preparing to release the arrow to pierce someone's heart with truth—just as the words on the pendant pierced my heart. *That's the gift we have to share with others.* Sharing our perspectives broadens theirs. We get glimpses of the world we wouldn't have seen on our own.

You belong here. The key is finding your purpose, or what calls you to create, and allowing the universe to expand to give it space and support it. *Listen to your inner voice.*

To create your own, individual path requires courage. In a world with many pressures to conform, it is heroic to be true to yourself and your values. When I am true to myself, energy flows through me and buoys me. When I am not true to myself, the flow is blocked, and I sink into confusion.

Being in touch with and aligned with your own inner compass is essential to the authenticity of your art—and your life.

CHAPTER 22

Take Compassionate Ownership

I started on my Creative Heroine's Path before it had a name, before I knew if I could even follow it. I've battled inner dragons again and again. It has not been easy, but it's been real, and profound. It's what we're all here for: to find our paths. When we lose track of them—and we will—we can find our way back, one step at a time.

Compassion is a bridge to connection, and a conduit for information. When you are stuck in negative self-talk, self-compassion allows you to soften—like a warm wind breaking up an ice floe—so that you can reenter the dance of creative expression, where new ideas and thoughts are available to you.

Compassion for yourself and others is an active state of being. It supports the level of honesty needed to live an authentic life with integrity. It is supported by the belief that each person is doing the best she is able, at any moment—including yourself.

Taking compassionate ownership of your life allows you to consciously act as the author of your life, without beating yourself up over your mistakes.

CHAPTER 23

Stories You Tell Yourself

As you create your path, you will tell yourself stories about it. Whether you interpret what happens to you with the focus on the positive or the negative is up to you.

A story is context, detail, and structure. We tell stories to ourselves to make sense of our lives and what happens to us. It's as normal as breathing.

Are the stories you're telling yourself supporting you—as stories are meant to do—or are they interpreting the events in your life in a way that keeps you stuck in roles and ways of being that don't serve you?

We're like ravenous detectives all the time, piecing together stories from incomplete information. Sometimes we get it right. Other times we don't.

There is necessary tension between what we most want to believe and what we most fear is true. In the borderland between the two, our highest aspirations and our deepest betrayals fight for a balance between idealism and cynicism.

To illustrate, I'll take you through a story you might be familiar with, from the movie *Casablanca*.

In World War II, Rick owns a bar in Casablanca. Some years earlier, in Paris, he fell in love with Ilsa. Ilsa left him right before they were to leave Paris, to escape the Nazi invasion, but she didn't tell him why.

Lacking the information he needed to complete the story, he believed that she had never loved him, and had in fact betrayed him.

Years later, when he sees her again in Casablanca, he learns the truth. Ilsa loved him, but found out just before their train was leaving Paris that her husband, Victor—whom she had believed was dead—was actually alive and very ill, after escaping a concentration camp. She couldn't leave him, and knew that if Rick knew the truth, he would stay behind to help. But Rick was wanted by the Gestapo, so she let him think the worst of her, to save him.

This is a classic example of making up stories—often based on our fears—when we don't have all the information. Ilsa was not only innocent, but she also sacrificed her relationship with Rick to do the right thing—and hurt him to save him. This was quite a different story from the one Rick had told himself.

Whenever one of your negative stories threatens to derail you, be aware that it is a story you made up. Try prefacing your stories with, "When this happens, the story I tell myself is…"

This is a useful tool when you're stuck in a perspective or story that isn't serving you. Challenge your assumptions. Clarify which details are facts and which are opinions. After all, you are the author and the protagonist of your life.

What do you want to create?

Approaching it from this perspective is helpful in several ways.

It's clean. You take responsibility for the story you tell yourself, and how you feel as a result.

It removes some of the emotional charge, and therefore the grip the story has on you, so you can bring more objectivity into the picture.

It reminds you to stay open and curious about the situation. You may be right, or partially right, or completely wrong. If you can let go of the need to be right to feel safe, the story may soften and change. It may not, but you'll never know unless you give it a try.

It helps you be aware of the bigger story you're living at the moment, giving you potential insights that help you shift your story from one that keeps you stuck to one that brings you more freedom.

It is respectful of the other person, if someone else is involved. When you project your story onto someone else's behavior, they get distracted by your story. If they feel attacked, they will defend themselves, rather than hearing you. But when you stay vulnerable enough to understand that you are telling yourself a story, based in part on your deepest fears (just like the other person may be), you have a better chance to discover a creative resolution.

Exercise: **Write One of Your Stories**

To practice finding the arc of meaning in your experiences, write your story in six paragraphs—one describing the experience you choose, and one for each of the five "acts."

1. The Experience—Choose an experience that was deeply meaningful to you.

   What is the context for that? The time frame?

2. The Change—Describe the change that happened.

   What was the catalyst?

   Was it inside of you, or something external that happened, or both?

3. The Call—What were you called to do?
4. The Challenge—What challenges did you face?
5. The Resolution—What treasures did you uncover?
6. Integration—How did you integrate the lessons you learned from this experience into your life?
7. With the hindsight of the lessons you learned, what would you call this story?

CHAPTER 24

Mastering the Path

Acceptance that you are not in control of everything helps you work with the flow, rather than against the current. Acceptance is not passivity; it is an active choice to trust, while you stay open to clues and intuition.

As you master the path, you become more adept at co-creating with the universe, and understanding the power of intention and trust.

Co-Creating with the Universe

Lately, I've been paying more attention to the effect of my intention on my experiences. A year before I completed this book, I taught a pilot program to a group of lovely women. Although I already had some material to use for the class, I wrote new versions each week, specifically for the program.

I was surprised to discover that each week, I experienced whatever phase in the path I was writing about.

In the week called "Diving into the Mystery," I struggled with writing the material. I felt lost and unsure of myself, my content, and my message. I was afraid that I didn't really know what I was doing.

I told myself I was a fraud, that I couldn't do it.

Who did I think I was, anyway?

Then I read the first words I wrote, in the original draft of *The Creative Heroine's Path*.

> "You know you've dived into the mystery when you feel alternately lost and found, hopeless and hopeful. You might experience a roller coaster of ups and downs, marinate in a stagnant soup, or twirl in a whirlpool. Round and round you go, until you finally find your still center, at the heart of the moving wheel that is your life."

Oh. Yeah.

It's amazing, really, how I experienced the material I was intending to write about, at a deeper level—which enriched what I ultimately had to offer.

I believe that when you have a clear intention, the universe "hears" you.

When you give the universe conflicting messages, it doesn't know how to work with you. When you are really clear on what you want to create—but you don't believe that you can do it, you hinder its manifestation.

> *"If ye have faith as a grain of mustard seed,*
> *ye shall say unto this mountain, remove*
> *hence to yonder place; and it shall remove;*
> *and nothing shall be impossible unto you."*
> Jesus
> (Matthew 17:20, American King James Bible)

You must remember that you are co-creating with the universe. The universe isn't an inert void, within which you must fight and scratch to get anywhere. It is alive, and it's made of meaning and metaphor as much as of chemical building blocks that can be translated to mathematics. Everything is connected.

What if everything you need already exists in the unmanifest world of possibility, and all you need to do is bring it forth?

Exercise: **Envision Your Life**

Describe one day in the life you envision for yourself, one year from now.

What do you really want?

Include:

- Your physical environment—structure and surroundings. Are you in a house, an office building, a city, the wilderness? What does it look like?
- Smells, aromas. Your favorite meal cooking, clean air, freshly mowed grass, lilacs, desert sage, city smells.
- The taste of the food you eat for at least one of your meals on that day.
- Sounds. Are birds singing outside your window? Is someone you love talking? Can you hear a train whistle in the distance? Waves pounding the shore? The hum of voices in a crowded room? A clock ticking in the hallway? Silence?
- Touch. The wood grain of the desk you're writing at. The handshake of someone attending your presentation. A hug from a child who benefits from your nonprofit. Moist soil in your hands. Soft fur of an animal you're caring for beneath your fingertips.
- Your sixth sense about it. What is there that you can't experience with any of your five senses? What do you just know?

The Creative Power of Intention and Trust

Intention is key. The magic of stepping up to try—committing to your vision and taking imperfect action—has shown up for me, over and over again, as I worked on the material in this book. I experienced each of the phases and processes I was writing about, simply by having the intention to focus on that specific phase or process.

Set an intention and act on it, without expecting perfection.

When I was living in Cincinnati, I decided to move to Boulder, Colorado. I had no family or friends there. I was a junior technical writer, and didn't have the money to relocate and then find work. So, every Tuesday at lunchtime, I stopped by the newsstand that carried the Sunday *Denver Post*, and bought a copy. I began to send resumés for open technical writing jobs in Boulder.

I didn't worry about it. I knew I would move. I was willing to put forth the effort needed, and to accept the amount of time it would take. It wasn't long before I got a phone interview with a company in Boulder. After that, they flew me out for an in-person interview. Then they hired me—and paid to move me there!

I moved to Colorado literally two weeks after my parents moved to a town a few hours away, where they were retiring to be close to their grandchildren.

My experience had a completely "meant-to-be" feeling about it. But I had the strong intuition that there was something about the way I approached the goal that made it happen so easily.

I believed it was possible. Even though I didn't know how it would work out, I trusted that it would.

I was clear about what I wanted to happen. I needed a job that would pay to relocate me.

I was excited about moving! There was real energy behind my intention. When I imagined how it would feel to be in a completely new place with mountain views, I felt happy.

I owned the commitment. I didn't just "want it to happen," I fully owned my part in making it happen. And when I did that, I knew I was going to move. No hesitation.

I accepted that I was not in control of everything. I put no time constraints on meeting my goal. Without the frantic time demands that

I have made in other circumstances—which actually seemed to block progress—I stayed calm and open.

I followed the flow. Because I stayed open to my intuition, I was able to follow the current to my destination, rather than trying to swim against the tide.

I did the work. I showed up, I made the effort, and I did my part to be able to jump into the flow and follow it. If I had waited for the flow to come to me, maybe a synchronicity could have showed up some other way, I'll never know. But a big part of "luck" is being in the right place at the right time, because you've done the work already.

Here's the thing: to invoke the magic of commitment, you must mean it, but you can't force it.

Tossing a Ball into the Universe

I think of my intention to move to Boulder like tossing a ball into the universe.

Think of the potential that exists in the unmanifest world. You put your intention out there, like tossing a ball. Your job is to do what's needed to put yourself in a position to catch it, when it's ready to come back down to earth.

You don't waste your time trying to control the ball once it's in the air; you adjust and act based on its trajectory. You "keep your eye on the ball."

You toss your vision into the universe, into the stream of time, and it manifests when you put forth the effort and conditions are right.

Walking Through the Magic Doorway

You might also call this the window of opportunity. It opens at the right moment. When it opens, you can leap through it enthusiastically, inch through cautiously, or hold back until it closes.

> *"There is a tide in the affairs of men.*
> *Which, taken at the flood, leads on to fortune;*
> *Omitted, all the voyage of their life*
> *is bound in shallows and in miseries.*
> *On such a full sea are we now afloat,*
> *And we must take the current when it serves,*
> *Or lose our ventures."*
> William Shakespeare

It always involves some sort of risk, something you have to give up in order to claim what is on the other side. What you have to give up may not be tangible. You may have to give up your attachment to doubt as a defense from potential disappointment.

You may discover that it was a mirage, or you didn't want what you thought was on the other side. But walking through the door of opportunity offers wisdom about yourself and the world, no matter how you judge the result of taking the risk.

Remember, you always have a choice of perspectives.

It is often only later, in hindsight, that you will know whether the choice—whether to walk through or stay put—was the choice you wish you had made at the time. Let go of the attachment to making the "right" choice. I've made choices that were right for me in the moment, but that my older, more experienced self would not have made.

Does that mean I made the wrong choice? Maybe. Sometimes. But hard choices are what help us learn who we are, and how the world is, to some degree.

If you're really stuck, try changing your perspective long enough to see through your confusion.

Ask yourself:

- If I don't take this path, how will I feel in five years? In ten? What does it feel like to be me in the future if I take the risk of staying put?

- If I do take this path, how will I feel in five years? In ten? What does it feel like to be me in the future if I take the risk of making this change?

Like me, your older self may have a different response in a few years, but this is the best way to get a glimpse of what it's like on each side of that doorway.

Using the Path as a Map

This path is a way of dancing in the moment, of being present in the world. Like me, you're on your own path, unique to you. But thanks to Joseph Campbell and others, we know that our experiences—both spiritual growth and creating art—follow a meaningful story arc. The path is like a blueprint of the organic process of transformation.

Consciously considering where you are on the path helps you keep the faith when you are lost. It helps you choose how to be and what to do in that space—to go deeper and move through, rather than staying stuck.

The universal story of innocence, loss, trials, wisdom, and sharing is our story. It's the nature of being human. Being lost and facing despair are necessary to finding ourselves and our inner wisdom. And this story structure not only applies to human life, it applies to whatever we attempt that requires spiritual growth: a piece of art, a novel, a new business, a relationship.

Over and over again, this is the story of creation. Of loss and becoming. Of making a life in this amazing world.

How does knowing the path support you? Here is an example.

The summer before my senior year in high school, I went on a road trip to the western United States with my aunt and uncle. We visited friends of theirs, who had a cabin in the foothills in Cody, Wyoming.

One afternoon, we hiked above the cabin until we came to a stream, then hiked beside the water for a while. When the others decided to hike back, I chose to linger. I sat on a rock, listening to the wind in the trees, loving the feeling of being alone in the mountains.

When I finally headed back to the cabin, I walked down beside the stream for a little while. I was unsure exactly where to move away from the stream to get back to the cabin. When I walked away from the stream, I saw only rocks and sagebrush.

That's when this Ohio girl began to think about bears and mountain lions, and being alone in what felt like the middle of nowhere.

Luckily, I knew enough to not wander too far from the stream. I kept walking, scared and worried I was lost the whole time. Finally, I crested a hill and saw the cabin below.

In your creative practice, and in your life, there are times when you lose your way. You don't know what you're doing or where you're going. Nothing can eliminate those moments; being lost is part of the process. On the other hand, having a structure and a story that provides context, and having a known path, can help you.

When you can't see past an obstacle (like the hill that obscured my view of the cabin), turn to what you know and understand of the path, to either remind you to trust the process, or help you determine which way to go.

Take Imperfect Action

Pick one thing that you can do in the next week to move forward, and do it.

Get the support you need. Join a writers group. Take a painting class. Hire a coach. Join the *Creative Heroine's Path* Facebook group.

Here's the truth: if it was easy, everyone would do it. You have to ask yourself if it's worth the effort to you. If it is, and you commit and do the work, you will create a work of art, or a new life, or whatever you want.

You can do it. Believe in yourself; I believe in you!

CHAPTER 25

Finding Grace

When I was near the completion of this book, a curious thing happened.

In the days before I was due to hand it off to one of the editors, I was in an emotionally tortured state, working long hours, afraid that it would not be good enough. This would be the first time that anyone other than myself was going to read the entire book, and I was sure I had so much more to do.

Even though I wanted more time to work on it, I honored the deadline. As a consolation, I planned to obsessively go over my copy again while the editor was looking at her copy. But instead, I let it go. I made the conscious choice to step out of trying to control my fear, and accept that my book was as good as I could get it at the moment. Whatever the outcome, I would deal with it.

When I met the editor to collect her comments, I learned that other than edits for clarity, she found no issues with my book. More importantly, it had done what I intended it to do: it had inspired her.

When I read through her edits, a deep calm spread through me. All that evening and into the next morning, I had a clear sense of myself—outside time, outside space, outside all the striving of life on this Earth.

This life we live is not who we are. It comes from who we are, to be sure, but it is not all there is.

I often get a sense of this in the early morning, when everything is blue, and quiet, and still. Then, the world begins to lighten like a stage. There is an expectant hush like the soft intake of a breath, until the imperceptible moment when night turns into day. Birds begin to sing. A man walks by with his dog. Somewhere, a car door slams. The damp smell of night sweetens slightly, as though flowers everywhere are opening their petals, turning their faces in anticipation toward the warmth of the rising sun.

This happens, in some form, every morning. Over and over, the world remakes itself. We awaken from the dream world of possibility, and begin to move as characters in a play, as the artists of our lives, attending to what is before us to make the possible real.

This was not the first time I'd experienced grace, nor will it be the last. I recognize grace as the moment of clearly seeing the eternal, what persists in all of us.

The morning after I met with the editor, I thought of Lily Briscoe, in *To the Lighthouse*. How, after years of carrying her vision of Mrs. Ramsay, she is finally able to finish the painting she had begun long ago. She sets her paintbrush down, and thinks to herself, "I have had my vision."

That is how I felt, too. I had a vision that I wanted to make real. And to share my vision, I had to become more visible. As I created my vision, it created me.

You have a vision, too. You can make it real. The elements in your life—right now as you read these words—are all you need to begin.

Remember your lodestar. Keep it close. It is a beacon from your soul to help you stay true to your Self, the part of you that is in the world, but not of the world.

Begin now. The world needs your gifts.

List of Exercises

Know What You Really Want 29
Develop Supportive Rituals 30
Discover Your Creative Assets 31
Know Your Allies 32
Celebrate Your Courage 33
Find Your Lodestar 35
Discover Your Perspectives 41
Choose Your Perspectives 43
Evaluate Your Perspectives 44
Practice Switching Lenses 51
Compare Victim and Creator Perspectives 52
Know Your Muse 63
Respond to Your Muse 66
Claim Your Creative Space 68
Declutter Your Space 72
Find Your Passion 79
Find Your Purpose 81
Find Your Power 83
Find Your Calling 85
Answer the Call 95
Recognize Your Inner Dragon's Magic Spells 111
Ground Your Energy 134
Keep Insights in Your Awareness 142
Find the Pearl 144
Check In with Your Vision 144
Create a Vision Board 147
Share Your Voice 167
Write One of Your Stories 177
Envision Your Life 180

Acknowledgments

No one does it alone. I am deeply grateful for the friendship and support of many people. I want to thank especially:

My husband, Dave Resch, for believing in me, battling my inner dragons (seriously, he deserves a superhero cape), and helping to publish this book.

My coach, Rick Tamlyn, for believing in my vision and holding me accountable to it, and for helping me get my message out into the world.

My editor, Risë Keller, for believing in me and helping me communicate my vision. (And by the way, I knew that "defuse" is not spelled "diffuse"—I was just testing you! Really.)

My proofreader for the second edition, Marsha Hippensteel, for catching the little things that can make a big difference.

My first reader, Lynn Weatherwax, for her feedback and reassurance that I'd communicated my vision.

My friend, Audrey Wilcox, for believing in me and cheering me on as I wrote this book.

My first life coach, Stephanie Collins, for helping me see possibilities when I believed there were none.

My dream analyst, Ron Masa, for being a touchstone to the hidden world, even years after we worked together.

And thank you to all the other people who acted as beacons for me in times light and dark, sharing their wisdom with the world.

Credits

Cover photo by soft_light/Shutterstock

Part 1: Welcome to the Path
  Mandala by Julie Baldwin

Part 2: Awakening Your Creative Spirit
  Sun Rising Over Green Hill by Julie Baldwin
  Lodestar by Julie Baldwin

Part 3: Dancing with the Muse
  Stars in Purple Cloud by Julie Baldwin
  Portrait de Jeanne Hébuterne by Amedeo Modigliani

Part 4: Responding to Your Calling
  Winged Heart by Julie Baldwin
  Arrow drawings by Ken West

Part 5: Diving into the Mystery
  Waves and Lighthouse by Julie Baldwin

Part 6: Sharing Your Gifts
  Flowers by Julie Baldwin
  Pine Trees with Figure in the Garden of Saint-Paul Hospital by Vincent Van Gogh

Part 7: Coming Home to Yourself
  House on Hill with Winding Road by Julie Baldwin

Author photo by Anna-Lee Baldwin Photography

About the Author

Julie Baldwin is a writer and painter who mentors soulful creatives to live more inspired and creative lives.

After 26 years in the corporate world, Julie left it all behind to pursue her creative calling. She began a quest to change her life, and to find and understand her own path for creative and spiritual growth. "I had to dive deep. I had to evaluate my long-held beliefs and perspectives. And I had to face my inner dragons and build my spiritual resilience."

Along the way, Julie learned that living a creative life means more than just expressing your creativity—it also means responding creatively to life's challenges.

The Creative Heroine's Path emerged from her experience. By looking at the creative process as a story, she illuminated the five phases in the creative flow. She learned to co-create in and from her life more consciously, because, she discovered, what we believe, we create.

Creative expression has always been an essential part of Julie's life. She has explored her creativity through writing, painting, drawing, photography, collage, printmaking, playing the piano, and singing.

Julie is a Certified Professional Co-Active Coach® (CPCC), and she has a certificate in Business Mastery from Inspired on Demand. She has a BA in English from Earlham College, and a MA in English from Wright State University.

Julie loves to write, paint, hike, read, take photos, travel, and ponder the mysteries of the universe. She lives in Colorado with her husband and a very spoiled Boykin Spaniel.

Learn more and read Julie's blogs at: JulieBaldwin.com

www.ingramcontent.com/pod-product-compliance
Lightning Source LLC
Chambersburg PA
CBHW051558010526
44118CB00023B/2745